Dino, Sheundar +

Something

together. Happy Chanuka

Jimmy

Pixie Folklore and Legends

Other titles from Random House Value Publishing

Celtic Myths and Legends
by Charles Squire

Irish Blessings

Scandinavian Folk & Fairy Tales

A Treasury of Irish Folklore

A Treasury of Irish Myth, Legend, and Folklore
by W. B. Yeats

Pixie Folklore and Legends

Originally titled
Piskey Folk: A Book of Cornish Legends

BY ENYS TREGARTHEN

COLLECTED BY ELIZABETH YATES

GRAMERCY BOOKS
NEW YORK • AVENEL

Originally published as *Piskey Folk: A Book of Cornish Legends.*

Copyright © 1940 by Elizabeth Yates;
copyright © renewed 1968 by Elizabeth Yates McGreal.
Foreword copyright © 1996 by Random House Value Publishing, Inc.
All rights reserved.

This edition is published by GRAMERCY BOOKS,
a division of Random House Value Publishing, Inc.,
40 Engelhard Avenue, Avenel, New Jersey 07001,
by arrangement with Elizabeth Yates
McGreal and HarperCollins Publishers, Inc.

Random House
New York • Toronto • London • Sydney • Auckland

Printed and bound in the United States of America

Library of Congress Cataloging-in-Publication Data

Tregarthen, Enys, 1851–1923.
[Piskey folk]
Pixie folklore and legends / Enys Tregarthen.
p.   cm.
Originally published: Piskey folk. New York : John Day Co., © 1940.
ISBN 0–517–14903–6
1. Pixies—England—Cornwall (County) 2. Legends—England—
Cornwall (County) I. Yates , Elizabeth , 1905–   . II. Title.
GR142.C7T7   1995
398.2'09423'7—dc20
95–24439
CIP

8 7 6 5 4 3 2 1

CONTENTS

FOREWORD

IN THE STAGE production of the children's classic *Peter Pan*, by J. M. Barrie, the audience's simple faith in fairies enables Tinkerbell to live. *Pixie Folklore and Legends*, a reprint of Enys Tregarthen's original text (published, posthumously, in 1940), functions in much the same manner: this enchanting collection of Cornish legends promises to preserve the magical world of fairies for a new generation of believers, old and young alike, for many years to come.

Enys Tregarthen was born in 1851 and lived, until her death in 1923, in a tiny village in Cornwall, collecting a multitude of Cornish legends and folk tales and creating children's stories all her own for which she is remembered fondly today.

Handicapped by a severe illness and bedridden at age seventeen, the young Tregarthen seems to have accepted the insularity of her physical world with an almost preternatural equanimity, turning, to our great fortune, to the world of imagination and fantasy for both inspiration and release.

Most nineteenth-century writers classified Cornish fairies into five distinct categories: the Knockers of the mines (descendants, many locals believed, of the Jews who were said, with no apparent substance, to have

FOREWORD

worked the mines in the time of the Druids), the
Brownies (held to be the guardians of the bees), the
Small People (spirits of an ancient Cornish race), the
Spriggans (a wicked and grotesquely ugly band of tiny
warriors), and the Piskeys (or Pixies), spirits of the
rivers, hills, and groves—mischief-makers who delighted in leading hapless travelers astray.

Yet, Tregarthen makes clear, Piskeys also concern
themselves with mortal affairs. Threshing the lucky
farmer's corn, cleaning a sick woman's house, and pinch-
ing the maidservant unfortunate enough to have left her
housework undone, Piskeys prove themselves the most
human of supernatural beings. Indeed, as in most myths
and legends, there are, in these delightfully fey stories,
more than a few grains of basic human truth. For, as old
Nance, in "Skerry-Werry" reminds us:
"Nobody is too dinky to have sorrow," . . . "an' even the
Small People must have their little sorrows, I s'pose."

In her lifetime "the little cripple," as she was affec-
tionately called, published a number of works, including
The Piskey Purse: Legends and Tales of North Cornwall
(1905), *North Cornwall Fairies and Legends* (1906),
and *The House of the Sleeping Winds* (1910). Two
decades after her death, the writer Elizabeth Yates edit-
ed and brought to publication this volume, originally
published as *Piskey Folk: A Book of Cornish Legends*
(1940), the introduction to which is included here.

2

FOREWORD

"The legends about the Little People are very old," the author wrote in 1906, "and some assert today that the tales about the Piskeys are tales of a pigmy race who inhabited Cornwall in the Neolithic Age, and that they are answerable for most of the legends of our Cornish fairies. If this be so, the older stories are legends of the little Stone Men. The legends are numerous. Some of them are fragmentary; but they are nonetheless interesting, for they not only give an insight into the world of the little Ancient People, but they also show how strongly the Cornish peasantry once believed in them, as perhaps they still do. For, strange as it may seem in these matter-of-fact times, there are people still living who not only hold that there are Piskeys, but say they have actually seen them!"

How fortunate to us, across the space of nearly a century, these beholders of Piskeys yet seem.

KATHRYN KNOX SOMAN

New York
1995

3

About the Editor

Elizabeth Yates has had a long and distinguished career as a writer and an editor of books for children and adults.

In 1951, she won the John Newbery Medal for *Amos Fortune, Free Man*. In addition, she has written many other charming works such as *Mountain Born, The Journeyman, Hue and Cry*, and *Someday You'll Write*.

GLOSSARY OF CORNISH WORDS

anist	near
austull	ceiling of boards
bal	mine
bare-ridged	bareback
bed-tester	the canopy of a bed
brandis	a three-legged iron stand used for supporting a pan or kettle over the fire
bufflehead	simpleton
cappry	goatlike
carns	rock-piles
cloam	earthenware
corncraik	a hand rattle used to frighten birds from sown seeds or growing crops
cricket	stool
croom	crumb
croom of a cheeld	a very small child
crowd	to fiddle
curley	curlew
diggle	miners' feast
dinky	very small
downs-organ	donkey
drexel	threshold
dummuts	twilight
durns	sideposts
flaygerries	frolics
God's little cow	the ladybird

GLOSSARY

googs	caverns
grig	cricket
gulph	rich vein
gunny	cavity
hawn	haven
horny-wink	plover
iss	yes
iss fy	by my faith
ivers	eyes, an exclamation of surprise
jinny-quick	grandmother's cap
joanies	small china figures
kibble	an iron mine bucket used for taking ore up a shaft
knocker	elvish miner
ling broom	a broom made of heather
long-cripples	vipers
moor cross	a Celtic cross used as a signpost
old men's learys	remains of old mining and stream works
pair	mining gang
rattle-bags	the capsules of the sea-campion
scaval-an-gow	confused chattering
seine	net
shag	cormorant
skavarnak	hare
skillywidden	Piskey baby
sloan	sloe, fruit of the blackthorn
slock-light	light of enticement
squills	wild flowers with pink, blue, and white blossoms
stumjack	stomach
thunder axe	Celtic tool

GLOSSARY

totties	pebbles
tor	high craggy hill
tributer	a miner who finds the ore and raises it to the surface
whiddle	tale
wisht	sad

INTRODUCTION

WHERE THE westernmost corner of England dips off to the sea is a land so different that it is called "the land outside England." Only the width of the Tamar river separates Cornwall from other English counties, but more than the flowing of water lies between. Cornwall's history goes far, far back, and, as it is held to in legends and stories, words and customs, the past lives on with almost as much reality as the present.

Cornwall is a land of rugged cliffs against which the Atlantic rolls, of sandy coves and little villages, of bare, windy moors, tin mines, white pyramidal heaps where the china clay is dug, and a race of people who share an enchanted quality with their land. From Tintagel in the north, where the old door opening onto the ruins of King Arthur's castle opens onto a world of romance, to the salty fishing towns in the south, the land between lies under an age-old charm: go through the little door, turn the pages of your fairy-tale book and—almost anything may happen.

Here, in this sunset land, the Arthurian legends grew and flourished. Here one may look across the sea to where the lost land of Lyonesse lies sunk beneath the waves and on soft nights hear bells ringing under the water or see the twist of a mermaid's tail. To this cragged coast the Celtic saints came to implant Christianity, sailing over from Ireland on a leaf or a millstone or in a bowl, building their churches and leading their lives of mingled fantasy and faith. Earlier still are tales of the Phoenicians coming here for tin, of merchants from Gaul; and earlier than that are the Druids and the little ancient men who first inhabited the land.

They have all left their marks: in the strange carns upon the hilltops, the hut circles, and old stones with their dark memories of pagan priests and mystic rites; in holy wells and Celtic crosses and churches worn gray with years but stalwart and beautiful; and they are all linked together in the tales one generation has left another.

Cornwall's own particular fairy folk are the Piskeys, and legends about them are as plentiful as sea shells. Living in the cliffs or on the moors, they were known to lead a prankish, but often useful, existence, always exceedingly merry. Some believe that they were once related to a pygmy race of Neolithic times; others hold to an earlier notion that they were Druids who resisted Christianity, and the more they resisted the smaller they grew. It was always thought they had lived before and "not good enough for heaven or bad enough for hell" remained on the earth. . . . Yes, Cornwall is a land where almost anything may happen, where legends brood and the past is hugged closely like a cloak.

In one of Enys Tregarthen's notebooks is a quaint explanation of the Piskeys.

"According to an old legend," she writes, "the Almighty went to call on Adam and Eve one day after they had been driven out of the Garden of Eden. When He arrived, Mother Eve was washing her children. She had not washed them all, for she had so many, and so she brought to the Lord only those that she had washed.

" 'Have you no other children?' the Lord God asked.

" 'No,' answered Eve, for she was ashamed to present to Him her little unwashed children and had hidden them.

"The Lord God was angry and said, 'What man hides from God, God will hide from man.'

"It came to pass as the Lord God had said, and all the unwashed children of the first mother became invisible. They went away into the hills, woods, forests, and lonely places of the earth and there took up their abode. They have remained invisible to the eye of man ever since, save to the few who have the faculty of seeing them or to those to whom they reveal themselves.

"These unwashed children of Eve are the fairies and are known throughout the world by different names.

11

"In Cornwall they are generally called Piskeys, but they have many other names too. Some call them the Small People; others the Dinky Men and Women or the Dinkies; some speak of them as the Little Invisibles. There are many kinds of Piskeys, such as the nightriders or the tiny people who ride horses and colts and even dogs by night; and the knockers or little miners who work and play down in the old mines. There are Spriggans, too, bad Piskeys with whom no one wants to have anything to do.

"These little invisible folk have their dwelling places on the wild downs and moors, by the side of streams, bogs, and marshes; on the great granite-piled hills; on the commons and cliffs and even down by the sea. They live in tribes or clans, each clan having peculiar qualities or characteristics, and though they show a common origin they differ considerably from one another."

The old Cornish people still tell tales of Piskeys, and through the years the stories have sometimes changed a bit, giving rise to different versions, sometimes lost a bit here or there. They might have been lost altogether but for the efforts of a few writers eager to perpetuate them.

Enys Tregarthen collected and wrote down many of the legends. Some were published in little books that are loved by story tellers and valued by students of folklore, and, though these books have long been out of print, many a library still treasures them upon its shelves. Now a whole new group of her stories has come to light, equally worthy of preservation.

Many years ago, Enys Tregarthen lived in the shipping town of Padstow on the north coast of Cornwall. The "little cripple" the country folk call her still, since most of her life was spent as an invalid. She loved Cornwall, and she loved the Cornish legends, and she did not want them to be lost, so she began writing them down—those she had been told as a child, and those she had heard from the old people whose memories seemed to go back to the beginning of time.

Whenever she learned of someone who had seen the Piskeys, she would ask that person to come and tell her about them. Sometimes it was a family story she would be told, like those of Jan Pendogget and Josey Tregaskis, similar to many another tale told in all parts of the country; sometimes it was a legend, hanging to the past by a frail, thin thread of memory, like the story of Bucca Boo.

A few of the tales have been folklore for ages, told in many versions all over Cornwall; others are peculiar to some spot, like The Piskey Warriors which was related by one of the natives of the Goss Moor who said she had both seen and heard the Piskeys. An old woman of ninety-four, named Rebekah French, who had often heard the story when a little girl, told of Alsey Trenowth and her broken promise, and, though she was never able to locate the exact spot where it had happened, she described it as an outlandish place on the moor.

An ancient dame of Davidstow was the very woman who was too curious, for it was in her own cottage that she had looked through the keyhole and seen the Piskeys cleaning her room and keeping it like a new pin. On the moors of the St. Columb district the legend of The Boy Who Played with the Piskeys was current. It was told to Enys Tregarthen by an old woman who said she put it as it was told her many years ago by a very old woman.

One day last summer when my husband and I were in Cornwall, we called upon a relative of Enys Tregarthen's. We told her of our love for the old tales and of our wondering if there could be others. It was a gray day; a rain-laden mist was sweeping in from the sea, and the wind was howling down the chimney. We had tea by the fire, a great steaming pot of it, some saffron buns, and "thunder and lightning"—that very special dish which is bread and Cornish cream and treacle on it. Then we were taken up to Enys Tregarthen's old room, one window of which looked out across the wide Camel River to the St. Minver sand hills, the other to the rocky tors of Bodmin Moor.

14

INTRODUCTION

A little trunk was pulled into the center of the room and opened before us. In it were scrapbooks, letters, and—more stories! They were bound in brown paper and neatly tied together, and all were written in Enys Tregarthen's careful hand. The paper had yellowed, in places the ink had faded and was not easy to read. There was a thick old smell of dust and all the years between, but the stories were fresh and glowing, filled with Cornwall. And while the wind blew and the rain swept against the windows, we sat on the floor and read the stories.

Here they are—legends and tales of Cornish folk and Cornish fairies on hill and moor and seacoast. We put them in your hands now.

ELIZABETH YATES

Pixie Folklore
and Legends

The Piskey
Revelers

ONCE UPON A TIME a Cornish youth was engaged to marry a Cornish maid, and he went to see her almost every evening when his day's work was done. The name of the youth was Benet Chegwidden, and the maid's Jenefer Kellaway. Benet lived at Porteath, a farm not far from the great headland of Pentire and within walking distance of Portquin, a beautiful little hawn on the north coast of Cornwall where Jenefer lived.

The youth was a farm laborer and the maid the daughter of one. He was tall and dark and a giant for strength, and she was small and fair. Her hair was the color of gorse blossom, and her eyes were the limpid brown of the stream that ran through the Trevigo Valley into the hawn.

The Kellaways' cottage faced the sea and near it ran the stream. It was a small cottage with a thatched roof, and its windows were filled with quarrels of glass as green as the water that ran under the cliffs at the flow of the tide. Pale green though they were, the quarrels glowed like fire when the evening sun shone upon them, making them look as if it were setting behind them instead of over the sea. Within the cottage were open

19

beams, a wide hearth, and a railed stairway leading to the bedchamber above. There was a settle, a small square table, a long bench, several fiddleback chairs, and an oak dresser. On the dresser stood an ancient pint measure which had belonged to Kitty Thorn, Jenefer's great-grandmother.

It was a queer old pint and had some mysterious connection with the Little People who visited the cottage every evening, so it was said. It seemed to know when its friends were waiting outside for it began to tap, tap, tap on the dresser. The Kellaways understood the meaning of these tappings for the minute the pint began to knock, Mrs. Kellaway would say, "The Little People have come, 'tis time for us to go upstairs," and no matter what time it was, or what they were doing, they climbed the railed stairway and never came down again till the morning.

The Kellaways did not mind being sent upstairs in this odd fashion, partly because they stood in some awe of the old pint measure, and partly because they did not want to prevent the Little People from coming to their cottage as they had been wont to do since the time of the great storm.

There is a tradition in the parish of St. Endellion, of which Portquin forms a part, that Portquin was once a big fishing place with many inhabitants and a large fleet. One day, when the men were out fishing in the bay, a storm suddenly arose, and every boat went down in the raging sea. Not a man was left, and soon the women forsook their homes and went inland. The forsaken houses crumbled away, and all but the more strongly built fell to pieces. The Cornish folk say that when places are forsaken by human beings the Piskeys come to live in them, taking possession of all that remains.

When the great storm was well-nigh forgotten, some farm laborers, among them the Kellaways, came to live in the hawn. They built up the walls of the houses still left standing, fitted them with thatches, windows, and doors, and made them habitable.

Benet Chegwidden was a frequent visitor at the Kellaways' cottage. He seldom arrived later than half-past seven when the days were long and seldom after six when they were short; but, sometimes, when there was much to do on the farm, he did not get to Portquin until close on nine o'clock. He was never late if he could help it for he wanted to be with brown-eyed, bright-haired Jenefer as long as possible, and he did not want to be sent away by the old pint measure the moment he had come.

The pint was no respecter of persons, not even of the good-looking youth who had walked all the way from

Porteath. Whether Benet had come early or late, when the pint began to knock and Jenefer said to him, " 'Tis time for 'ee to go, Benet, the Little People have come," Benet took up his hat, said good night and left.

But Benet, although he went obediently enough on most occasions, soon began to resent being dismissed in this arbitrary fashion.

One evening, when Benet happened to arrive unusually late, the pint started tapping the moment he crossed the threshold of the door. It made him so angry that he told Jenefer he would not be sent away the moment he came for all the Small People in Cornwall. Moreover, he declared that he had his doubts as to whether there were little bits of men and women, and he suspected that the old pint was anxious for him to be gone for some other reason best known to herself.

Jenefer was greatly distressed to hear her lad talk in this way.

"There be Little People," she said solemnly. "They are the ancient ones who lived in Cornwall in the days of the Druids. They came to our cottage before my great-granfer and great-granny lived here."

"And what do they come to do?" asked Benet.

"Why, to have their little flaygerries as they did after the storm when all the cottages belonged to them," Jenefer answered simply. "Mother an' me would not like

22

to prevent them from coming now, an' we shouldn't know when they wanted to come in if the pint didn't tell us."

"But you have never seen the Little People come into your cottage an' never seen them go," persisted Benet. "I haven't nuther, an' I have looked back to see if they were outside or down in the hawn when you and the old pint have sent me away."

"'Tis true that I haven't seen the Little People come into our cottage nor leave it," said Jenefer, "for I have never let my curiosity get the better of me. But I have sometimes heard the sound of little music and merry laughter when I have been upstairs in my bed."

The pint began to knock again, this time more impatiently.

"You must go," she urged. "We can't afford to offend the Small Folk, who have been friendly with us up till now. 'Tis lucky to have little bits of men and women come to a cottage as they do to ours, and unlucky when they are driven away from it. So, Benet, you *must* go!"

The earnest tone of her voice and the pleading in her eyes, more than her words, made him obey her; but there was resentment in his heart and undefined doubt in his mind as he went on his way to Porteath.

"If there be Little People who come into houses after sundown, I hope I shall see them some day," Benet muttered to himself. "I've heard the old grannie-women say that people get Piskey-eyed and may such be my good fortune, for I'm not a-going to believe what I cannot see no matter how many pint measures give me their orders."

It was the fall of the year now and the days shut in early. But Benet had much to do and often did not finish his work till late. One evening he wondered if it would be worth his while at all to go to Portquin, for if he got to the Kellaways' cottage when the old pint measure began to tap he would see Jenefer for scarcely more than a minute.

"But I'll just go round the cliffs all the same," Benet thought, "the walk will do me no harm."

He looked a handsome youth in his clean, white smock frock, corduroy breeches, and blue yarn stockings as he went toward Hipp Hawn cliffs. From there, a grander view in North Cornwall could hardly have been spread before him. To the right and left of him were mighty cliffs, and beyond him was Pentire with the waves leaping against its sides. The moon was full and hung like a hurler's ball in the cloudless sky, which was a deep dark blue like the mussels that cling to the rocks on the shore. The sea beneath the moon was glistering with light, and the water between Pentire and an island called The Mouls was a silver fire.

"The Sound of Mouls is brighter than a seine full of

24

pilchards," said the youth to himself. " 'Tis a quiet evening too, I can hear the waves rushing into the googs an' breaking on the beaches as plain as if I was down there."

He turned his back on Pentire and went toward Portquin, singing an old Cornish song, and as he sang his strong voice mingled with the thunder of the breakers over the smooth sands below the cliffs on which he walked. He strode over the Top o' Lundy till he came to a place known as Moon's Ground and suddenly stopped his singing, thinking he heard on the cliff side of him thin, gay laughter. He looked around but saw nothing that could have caused it.

" 'Twas a herring gull laughing in his sleep," Benet said aloud.

Moon's Ground was a beautiful spot in the daytime with its heather and gorse and golden samphire, but it was weird enough after sunset. The place was full of dark green mounds, called Piskey dwellings by the old people, and tiny roads soft as velvet that ran all the way to Tintagel and even further.

Benet looked around him uneasily, then started on his way. He had gone only a few steps before he stopped again, this time at the sight of a coach about the size of a large turnip coming out of one of the mounds and going like the wind in the direction of Portquin. It came out of the mound quietly and rolled away even more quietly so that a moment after it was gone Benet could not be sure whether he had seen anything at all. He went on his way, but this time he did not sing till he reached Trevan Point, another headland dark and somber like Moon's Ground.

It was a wild garden in which grew vernal squills, lady's-fingers, and many another cliff flower. Mosses grew here too, and lichens encrusted the rocks thrust out of the ground, most of them as yellow as spade guineas. Seabirds had their dwelling places in the cliffs, and Benet, who had crossed Trevan Point times untold, had often heard them laughing and whistling. This evening, however, his ears were greeted by other sounds—rolling wheels and squeaky voices. He looked about him to find the cause of the sounds and thought he saw shadowy forms low on the ground, each one carrying a tiny light.

Benet was brave enough, but the sight made him feel distinctly nervous. All the tales he had heard about the Little People who live in the cliffs and moors came back to him as the mysterious lights bobbed to and fro. He quite forgot that only a little while ago he had told Jenefer he did not believe there were such things as dinky men and women. He even forgot he had said that if there were such creatures he would like to see them.

Then suddenly it flashed across his mind that he had become Piskey-eyed.

"I don't want to see them after all," he said to himself. "I'll go back from the cliffs out of their way."

Leaving the cliffs he went over a small common and soon came to a steep hill called Doyden Hill which led down to Portquin. Whistling now for courage's sake, he went down the hill. But he had not gone far when, to his dismay, he saw a long string of tiny coaches slowly descending the hill in front of him. They were like the coach he thought he had seen coming out of the mound at Moon's Ground, only as these were going slowly he could see them more distinctly.

They were beautiful coaches, each a different color and drawn by horses no bigger than an eight weeks' kitten. Behind every coach stood a man in a red coat, green hat and breeches, and red stockings, while a man similarly dressed sat on the box seat driving.

"My dear senses!" Benet exclaimed, rubbing his eyes to make sure he saw aright. "I've heard my old Granny Chegwidden say that the Little People drove about in coaches, but I didn't believe it before, no fy I didn't! And I didn't believe there was such little bits of men and women like Jenefer said there was, but I believe it now!"

He had hardly said this when out from the hedge,

which lay in shadow, sprang an odd-looking person about five inches tall, wearing a pointed cap. He had immense ears, a thin sharp face, and no neck to speak of, and his body and legs seemed too small for his ears. The sight of this weird man so startled Benet that he backed into the opposite hedge just as a tiny coach and four, prancing white horses in green trappings driven by a coachman in green, passed on its way down the hill. As it went by, Benet saw two lovely faces not much bigger than sixpenny pieces looking out of the window.

The coach had no sooner rolled by than dozens of others passed on their way down the hill; each one was more beautiful than the last, and in every one Benet saw tiny men and women. The last was a golden coach and six with scarlet trappings like a State coach. The driver and the footmen were clad in scarlet and gold, but Benet did not see the Little People inside as they were not looking out. Behind this came a crowd of men and women on foot, talking and laughing one to another, their voices round and sweet like the chirps of geese-chicks soon after they come out of the shell.

These were followed by a company of musicians, fiddlers with their fiddles, flautists with their flutes, reed players with their reeds, horn players with their horns. Some of them looked like the five-inch man who had sprung from the shadows. Some of them were in red, some in green, others wore jackets and some wore cloaks, but all had sugar-loaf hats and pointed shoes that reached almost to their knees. Benet hardly breathed till this crowd had passed. When it had reached the bottom of the hill, he took off his hobnailed shoes and walked down the road in his stockings.

"I must see where the Little People be going," he said to himself, "for they're going to hold a revel somewhere, 'tis plain as a weathercock. Surely they can't be going to hold it in the cottage where my dear little maid do live, there are too many o' mun for that."

When Benet reached the hawn, he saw the coaches going over a rustic bridge which spanned the stream, while all the tiny people waited by the bridge. The evening was still fine, and the sky without a cloud. The moon was flooding the hawn with radiance, making everything visible. The sea in the open bay was a silver glitter but black as ebony under the cliffs. The tide was out, and the uncovered pebbly beach was bright like the bay.

Benet stood at a distance from the stream but near enough to see what the Little People were doing. When the last of the coaches was over and the last musician had crossed, he came and stood by the brink of the stream to see where they were going. Up to the door of the Kellaways' cottage rolled the long line of dinky coaches; then the gentlemen began helping the ladies out of the coaches, and the elegant way they did it was past believing.

"An' every one o' mun dressed up to the nines in velvet and silks, an' their little breeches fastened with buckles that glitter like the sea-washed totties on the beach," Benet commented admiringly. "An' as for the little ladies no higher than my thumb, with their gowns as soft as flowers, they be that handsome I don't wonder the gentlemen like to bow an' scrape before them as they be doing, no fy I don't!"

Each gentleman led his lady to the cottage door and disappeared, but how Benet did not know for the door was shut. When the coaches were empty, the coachmen flicked their whips and drove up the valley and were lost in the shadow of the trees. Then the Little People who had come to the hawn on foot went into the cottage, and as Benet looked closer he saw the fiddlers roll themselves as small as marbles and roll under the doorway, the flute players climb up the durns of the door and go through the keyhole, until there was not a dinky body to be seen anywhere.

There was no light in any cottage in Portquin that Benet could see, but some of the cottage windows facing the cliffs reflected the shine of the moon. There was no sign of human life in the hawn for everybody was in bed.

30

Neither was there any sound save the wash of the sea on the beach, the swish of the water in the googs, and the ripple of the stream.

"I wonder if I may make so bold as to peep in at the window of Jenefer's cottage an' see what the Little People be upon?" thought Benet. "I told my maid that I didn't believe there was such creatures, an' since my unbelief has come back upon me I would like to be able to tell her that I not only saw them go into her house but saw them there!"

He crossed the bridge and drew near the Kellaways' cottage. "I don't suppose the little dears will mind my looking through the window at all since I was fortunate enough to see them coming down Doyden Hill."

He stood by the window, his eyes glued to its small green panes. For awhile he saw nothing, then gradually he became aware that the room was lit with a soft light and that sounds of music filled his ear. Then he saw hundreds of Little People standing around the room, each gentleman with his lady, watching about a hundred others dancing. At one end of the room, facing the window, were two people sitting on a cricket. They were dressed in robes that sparkled like dewdrops on gossamer, and on their heads were crowns which glittered still brighter than their robes.

"The King and Queen of the Little People, I suppose,"

31

Benet murmured. "Wouldn't Jenefer open her pretty brown eyes wide if she knew there was royalty in her father's and mother's cottage?"

Benet could hardly take his eyes from the grand little bodies on the cricket, but when he could he watched the dancers, who seemed to be doing some intricate dance for they went in and out and round about till his head began to swim. To prevent himself from getting dizzy, Benet turned his gaze to the gentlemen and their ladies standing around the room. And he, who had never failed to show his brown-eyed Jenefer those little attentions every girl expects, was delighted to see what attention the dinky gentlemen were paying their ladies.

"I don't believe our Squire up to Roscarrock *could* pay his lady more attention than these little bits of gentlemen be paying these tiny ladies," thought Benet.

While the lad was watching every movement of the dancing folk, a queer tapping came from the dresser. Benet turned and saw that the old pint measure was dancing for all it was worth, knocking out the tune the musicians were playing. How the pint was footing it, Benet could not tell as it had no feet that he could see. Up and down the dresser it went, twisting and twirling like the dancers on the floor below. As it turned, Benet saw on the smooth surface under its spout a weird face with a wink in its eye and a broad grin on its mouth, something like the face of the odd-looking man who had jumped out of the hedge when Benet was coming down Doyden Hill.

"I believe the old thing dancing away like a pickled herring at a fair is a Piskey turned into a pint measure," cried Benet, forgetful of how he had once felt toward the pint.

"Dance a little faster, booby," called a shrill voice.

Benet saw that the little musickers were now all standing on the dresser shelves, except for some three or four fiddlers who were sitting on the edge of the top shelf with their legs dangling, fiddling away as hard as they could. The small players, for not one was over six inches tall, were playing with all their might, making faces as they played. One stood fiddling away with his head on one side, his little stumjack thrust out and his bit of a foot beating time.

"A Christmas play is nothing to it," said Benet. "However did the dinkies learn to play like that, I do wonder. Old Fiddler Moyle down Portyssick Hawn can't crowd half so well. The dinky crowder here would take the shine out of all the crowders in Endellion, iss fy he would!"

Little People, like human beings, cannot go on dancing forever, and those in the Kellaways' cottage suddenly stopped, and so did the pint measure. The musicians ceased to play, and Benet half expected the old pint would return to its usual stolidness after the dancing was over, but it did nothing of the kind. Coming to the edge of the dresser, it bent over, and, as it did so, one of the little ladies came over and talked to it. What she said Benet could not hear, though her words must have pleased the pint for it seemed to shake with laughter and grow visibly brighter till it glowed like a warming pan in the light of the fire.

"That old pint is a proper old flint," laughed the lad.

When Benet next looked at the Little People, he saw that most of them were sitting on the floor, which was covered with something soft and green. Small men that looked like waiters were carrying around trays laden with hedge fruit and cakes. Most of the folk were holding glasses no bigger than moss cups, and the plates in their laps were the size of daisies. Whether it was wine or water Benet could not tell, he knew only that it was full of sparkle when the glasses were held up to the light. Where the light came from was another mystery to him. He had often seen hedges glimmering with glowworm lights on his way back from Bodmin on a summer's night, and the soft pale light in the room made him think of them.

As the large company of Little People were eating and drinking, talking and laughing, the fiddlers and the other musicians began to play again. It was not dance music this time but soft music that made Benet think of faraway bells and the dripping of water, notes of young birds and the sighing of wind among the elders out on the moor. The tiny voices and silvery laughter of the folk as they feasted seemed a part of the music, and Benet felt as if he could have listened forever.

Then, after how long Benet never knew, the King on his cricket gave a sign. The Little People rose from the floor. The musicians put away their instruments. The rolling wheels of the coaches could be heard coming through the hawn. The merrymaking was over and the guests were going home. Benet clung to the sight of them until the last one had disappeared up the curves of Doyden Hill, then he turned around for one more glimpse of the room that had seen such gaiety.

The moon was coming into the cottage in a long beam of silver, and the sight that met the lad's eye filled him with dismay. For the spry old pint was not on the dresser shelf, not on the table, but lying forlornly on its side on the hard stone floor.

"Poor fellow, perhaps 'ee had too good a time," sighed Benet sympathetically. "Whatever will my Jenefer think when she sees 'ee so?"

Benet had quite forgot the resentment he had felt against the old pint when, on more than one occasion, its tapping had sent him home. He thought only how grieved Jenefer would be when she discovered it in the morning on the floor.

So, with no more noise than the moon made as it entered the cottage, Benet pushed the door open and stole softly across the floor. He picked up the old pint, brushed it off, and fondled it tenderly, then put it in its place upon the shelf. Before shutting the door of the cottage, Benet looked back at the pint. The moon was full on it, burnishing its smooth surface, and just for a moment the pint smiled back at the youth as broadly and merrily as when it had been footing it up and down the dresser.

Benet crossed the bridge quickly and went up the hill with long strides, but by the time he reached Porteath the moon had set and the morning star was rising in the pale blue sky.

The next night when Benet called on Jenefer, and all the other nights until they were married and went to live in their own cottage, he stayed as long as he had a mind to, for it was only after he had closed the door behind him that the tapping of the old pint measure gave the signal for the nightly gathering of Little People.

Skerry-Werry

ON A GREAT wind-swept moor in King Arthur's country stood a gray stone cottage with a shaggy roof of straw. The cottage was occupied by a widow woman named Nance Pencarrow. Nance was up in years, but in spite of her age her heart was young and she loved children dearly. She was also fond of animals, especially of her golden cat whom she called Tommie Cat.

The moor was a lonely spot, but Nance had gone there when she was first married, and now she was old she did not want to live anywhere else. Besides, she was too busy to feel the loneliness for she had to get her own living which she did by spinning wool and flax.

When her day's work was done and she had had her supper, she went outside her cottage to enjoy the view. The moor was beautiful to her in all seasons and in all weathers, but particularly so at sundown when the setting sun made the brown moorland streams like rivers of gold.

One evening late in the summer, when the moor was like amethyst fire with heather, there was an unusually fine sunset. The sky behind the sinking sun was a background of pale yellow on which stood out, in sharp relief,

37

great clouds of all wonderful shapes and sizes and every color. Nance watched, enchanted, until the sun was a mere speck on the distant, glittering sea. She was so charmed that she never thought of going into her cottage till the last glimmer of the afterglow had pulsed out of the sky and the stars began to show themselves.

The night seemed unnaturally dark after such splendor, and, as the old woman turned to go in, she was startled to hear a little voice piping, "I've got no mammie to mammie me. Oh dear, what shall I do?"

"My dear senses!" Nance ejaculated. "Whatever is that crying?"

The voice, small as it was, seemed to fill all the silence, and the despair in it went straight to the old woman's kind heart. She listened intently but could not tell whence the cry came. One minute it seemed to be on her right, the next on her left, then it seemed to be away in the distance.

"The little mammieless thing is like a quail, you never can tell where it is," said Nance to herself as the tiny voice once more piped its mournful pipe.

"I'll go in and light my lantern and try to find the poor little cheeld," said the old woman as she hastened into the cottage. Entering it she noticed that her fire had burned down, so she poked it into a blaze, threw on furze and turf, lit her lantern, and went out again on to the moor. The fire leaped and flamed as she went and sent a warm glow after her through the open door.

"Where be 'ee, my little dear?" called the old woman, holding her lantern close to the ground.

As she held it the tiny voice wailed out again, "I've got no mammie to mammie me. Oh dear, what shall I do?"

Nance looked down and close to her feet, on a small bank of wild thyme, was a white face set in a frame of wind-blown hair. Tiny as the eyes were, Nance could see that they were blue as bluest milkworts.

"Why, you be a little bit of a cheeld!" cried Nance astonished. "You be that small 'twas no wonder I couldn't see 'ee. How did 'ee get out here on this lone moor all by your little self?"

The tiny creature with shining hair and blue eyes made no answer but again wailed out, "I've got no mammie to mammie me. Oh dear—"

"Where is your mammie?" interrupted Nance in great concern. "Shame upon her to leave 'ee in this lone place, if she did leave 'ee," Nance added as the child did not speak. "You be a little woman-cheeld by the looks of 'ee."

"I've got no—" began the tiny voice once more while the pathos in it filled Nance's kind heart with pity.

"I shall mammie you if you will let me," she said, going down on her knees beside the little creature. "I shall dearly love to mammie you for I have nothing of my own to love except Tommie, my cat, an' the little moor birds."

"Will you really mammie me?" asked the child softly.

"Iss fy, I will, the same as if you was my own cheeld. You shall lack for nothing if I can help it."

"Then you shall mammie me till you can't hold me on your lap," said the child.

"That's a bargain," cried Nance, smiling all over her comely old face. "Come along with me into my cottage an' warm your dinky self by the fire."

The tiny creature tripped lightly after the old woman into the cottage. At the door they were met by the big golden cat, who held his tail aloft and purred loudly.

"Tommie Cat is pleased to see 'ee," said Nance in great delight. "He is a very particular gentleman an' don't like anybody except his ould mistress. So you must be in his good graces."

The child, who was not much taller than the golden cat when he stood on his hind legs, went straight to the fire and sat down on a small cricket. Tommie Cat sat by her side and purred yet more loudly while Nance gave the child a slice of buttered brown bread and a cup of goat's milk.

The little maid took it gratefully. When she had eaten

40

and drank, she looked up at Nance and said, "Please, what must I call you?"

"Call me Mammie Pencarrow, if you please, my dear," returned the old woman.

"I will," replied the child. "Now, will you take me upon your lap and mammie me, Mammie Pencarrow?"

"Gladly," cried Nance, and seating herself in her elbow-chair she lifted the tiny creature onto her ample lap.

"My dear life, how heavy you be!" she exclaimed. "Whoever would have believed you was such a lump of a cheeld!"

The old woman, holding the child, petted her and called her by every endearing name she could think of till the fire died down and the cat began to mew.

"Tommie Cat thinks 'tis time we was in bed," said Nance at last. " 'Tis just upon midnight, I reckon."

"I never sleep in a bed," said the child. "I sleep on the heather."

"I picked some heather only yesterday to dry for my fire," replied Nance. "I shall make a bed with it in the corner of my little chamber, an' I'll cover 'ee over with a quilt which the Small People made for my ould grand-mother's firstborn."

"Then I shall be snug and warm," said the child, "and safer than little moorbirds under their mothers' wings."

Nance made haste to make a bed of heather, then she

41

took the quilt from a chest, and soon the tiny stranger was lying fast asleep under the coverlet which was many-hued like the bow in the cloud and almost as soft. The child did not sleep long, and almost before the larks left their nests in the dewy turf she was awake, merry as a grig with her talk and laughter.

All that day Nance could hardly spin for watching the child dancing, until at last she exclaimed to her, "You can dance like the Dinkies!"

"Did you ever see the Dinkies dance?" the child asked quickly.

"No, but my ould grannie did," Nance replied. "I sometimes wish I had the gift of second sight as she had."

"Do you?" cried the little maid. "Perhaps you will grow new eyes, Mammie Pencarrow, and see even more wonderful things than your grannie saw."

When evening came Nance put aside her spinning wheel and got the supper ready for herself, the child, and Tommie Cat. After they had eaten, all three went to the door of the cottage and looked out over the great moor. The child soon got tired of standing still and began to dance like a gnat in the sunshine. As twilight spread over the earth the child ceased from her dancing and gazed toward the east where great boulder-crowned hills stood up against the evening sky.

"Be 'ee looking for your mammie?" asked Nance, noticing her eager gaze.

"No, I am looking for something I think you will like to see. It is traveling fast over the moors from the tor country. Look, Mammie Pencarrow, look."

Mammie Pencarrow looked but saw nothing save the will-o'-the-wisp. "I can see nothing but Piskey lights whipping along," she said laughing. "I have seen Piskey lights times without number."

"Look, all the same," begged the child, "and keep your eyes fixed on the first light."

The old woman did as she was bidden and saw a teeny tiny white hand holding a lantern the size of a sloan.

"My goodness gracious," Nance exclaimed, "if my ould eyes didn't deceive me, I saw a dinky hand holding a teeny tiny light flip by my door. 'Twas a lovely little hand, sure 'nough, an' white as a moon daisy."

"You have begun to grow new eyes," laughed the child, clapping her hands.

"The dinky hand must be the hand of a Little Body like my ould grannie used to see," said Nance. "How I wish I could see the rest of her!"

"You will see lots of wonderful things if you get new eyesight," the child murmured.

The following evening again found the old woman,

the little maid, and Tommie Cat outside the cottage. The child danced till the sun had set and the stars were reflected in all their silvery whiteness in the moorland pools. Then the dancing ceased, and the child sent her glance toward the tor country.

"There is something coming along," she said softly. "It will be here in a minute. Look hard at it when it comes near."

The old woman looked hard. When it came close to the cottage she exclaimed, "My dear life, I see two dinky feet dancing along! The feet do match the hand I saw yesterday eve. What darling little feet they be!"

"They are dancing like the Dinkies you told me about yesterday," said the child. "Oh, I am so glad you have seen the little feet for now I know that you are growing new eyes."

The next day it was wet. The rain fell quietly on the moor, bringing out the fragrance of the wild thyme, the mints, and many another moorland plant till the great open space with its multitude of flowers was full of sweetness.

"I'm afraid the Piskey lights won't come whipping over the moor in the dummuts this evening for 'tis raining an' will rain till tomorrow if I can tell the weather," said Nance as she sat at her spinning wheel and watched the child playing with the yellow cat. "An' I do so want

44

to see the Little Body. I want to see her all to once unless she goes about in bits!"

The rain did not leave off, and the sun went down behind gray clouds. At eventide, when they went to the door and looked out, there was nothing to be seen save a heavy veil of mist.

"The mist is as thick as a hedge," said Nance. "We may as well go in an' sit by the fire."

"We will," cried the child, "and you shall hold me on your lap."

When the old woman had taken her seat in the elbow-chair she took the child on her lap, but to her astonishment she found her grown heavier. "Why, if you get much heavier I shan't be able to hold 'ee," Nance exclaimed. "I can't understand how you're such a great weight. You en't growing no bigger nuther. If my ould eyes tell me true, you have gone smaller!"

The child laughed mischievously.

"Somebody must have stepped over 'ee when you was a croom of a baby," Nance went on, "or you have stepped over a ling broom. If that was the case, you will always be a little go-by-the-ground like the Small People." Then she added tenderly, "but you will always be a little skerry-werry."

"What is a skerry-werry?" asked the child.

"A little body, quick an' light on her feet," said the

45

old woman, "an' you be ever so quick on your dinky feet. I think I shall call 'ee Skerry-Werry."

"Do," said the child, "it is a nice name. Now, sing to me, Mammie Pencarrow, sing to Skerry-Werry."

Nance began to sing, but her voice was so loud and harsh that the cat left the hearthstone and jumped up on the window seat, and the child put her hands over her ears.

"My voice is harsher than corncraiks," said the old woman, "but I was willing to oblige 'ee, my dear. Sing to Mammie Pencarrow instead, won't 'ee now?"

Nothing loath, the little maid opened wide her red mouth and began to sing. Her voice was so bewitching that the old woman could not keep still. Her head went niddle noddle, her hands tried to keep time to the tune, the crock on the brandis went twirling, and the cloam on the gaily painted dresser started to dance, the cricket tapped on the floor, and Tommie Cat stood on his legs in the window seat.

"Stop singing, I beg of 'ee," Nance implored, "or I don't know what will happen. My little house will go dancing away over the moor unless 'ee stop."

The child stopped but she seemed surprised. "Was my voice harsh as a corncraik's?" she asked.

"No fy, it wasn't, I never heard such singing in all my life, but what it was about I have no more idea than

Tommie Cat. You sang in a strange language, my dear, there wasn't a word of Cornish in it!"

The day that followed was a beautiful one. Skerry-Werry danced till Nance's head went spinning like her wheel and the big golden cat sat on his tail and looked amazed. At the setting of the sun all three went out on the moor. The child did not dance and the cat was as still as if he were sitting by a mousehole. The twilight came quickly after the sun had dropped into the sea.

"The Piskey lights have left the tor country," the child said. "Look, Mammie Pencarrow, look."

The Piskey lights came nearer and nearer. When they were quite close, Nance saw a teeny tiny woman about the height of her thumb at the head of the lights. Her face was white and shiny like a wren's egg fresh from the nest, her hair was as yellow as a sunbeam and as silky as cotton grass. Her dress was green and all of a glimmer like glowworm light. In her hand she held a lantern the size of a sloan, and the light that came from it was as silvery as the dew's crystal beads. She smiled as the old woman gazed down at her when she whipped past.

"My dear soul an' body, what a lovely little lady!" Nance exclaimed. "She must have been one of the Small People my ould grannie used to see."

"I'm ever so glad you have seen a Dinky," cried

47

Skerry-Werry. "You really are getting your grand-mother's gift, Mammie Pencarrow, the gift of second sight."

"There's more Piskey lights traveling over the moor," said the old woman, and keeping her gaze fixed on them she saw a teeny tiny horse's head with a golden mane which the head tossed as it flew by the cottage.

"My dear senses, whatever shall I see next?" laughed Nance with the glee of a child. "Now I wish I could see the rest of the little horse, his little tail and all! He must be a handsome critter judging by his head."

"I'm so glad you have seen the head of a dinky horse," piped the child, "for now I am certain that you have grown your new eyes."

For a long time they kept their faces turned toward the east, but they saw no more that night, and when the dummuts changed to darkness they went into the cottage.

The next evening, when the sun had gone under the water, the old woman faced the tor country to watch for Piskey lights. For a long time she watched in vain, then out of the twilight appeared four tiny lights which came galloping over the ground. When they came near she saw four horse's feet.

"I expect 'tis the feet of the dinky horse whose head I saw last night," cried Nance, holding up her hands.

48

"I wonder what you will see next," said Skerry-Werry.

"I wonder," echoed the old woman.

The next day it was misty, but for heat and not for rain. The mist lay white as hoar frost on the turf and heather, and the great hills were wrapped in gray.

"This sort of weather won't prevent the Piskey lights from whipping about if they're so minded," said Nance as she sat at her wheel.

"They will be minded, Mammie Pencarrow."

"How do you know, Skerry-Werry?" Nance asked.

"Because you mammied me," was the answer.

The moment supper was over and the things put away, Mammie Pencarrow, Skerry-Werry, and Tommie Cat went outside the cottage. The setting sun shone behind a thin veiling of mist. Through an eyelet in the fog could be seen the curve of the new moon. The evening was hot and sultry even on the open moor.

"I fear there won't be anything out of the common for my ould eyes to see tonight," said Nance.

"Perhaps not for your *old* eyes to see, but there may be something lovely for your *new* eyes."

As Skerry-Werry was speaking, out of the mist came a teeny tiny prancing horse as bright as the crescent moon, with a golden tail that swept the ground. He was not half so big as Tommie Cat, but he was perfect, bare

49

as a colt and as full of life and grace. His golden mane flew out as he came, and he galloped so fast that he was out of sight almost as soon as they saw him.

"My dear heart alive, I have seen the whole of the dinky horse!" Nance exclaimed. "Whoever would have believed there were such things as horses not so big as Tommie Cat!"

"It isn't everybody who can see a dinky horse," said Skerry-Werry. "Not one in a million. But the fog is lifting, and in the clearness I can see something coming. Look, Mammie Pencarrow, look."

Nance, sending her glance to where the child pointed, saw a long train of golden light coming over the turf. The cat shot out his ears, and his eyes became balls of green fire. The light was many yards in length and out of it appeared a hundred tiny horses. On every horse rode a tiny horseman dressed in a bright green coat and breeches and a red hat.

The old woman was too astonished to utter a word and sat, staring, with her eyes and mouth wide open. Behind the horses, which all had long manes and sweeping tails, came a teeny tiny carriage drawn by twelve horses as white as ewe's cream. In the carriage sat a teeny tiny woman with a very sad face. She looked so sorrowful that Nance's kind eyes filled with tears. As she gazed at her, the golden carriage and the prancing horses were almost lost sight of in her pity for the sad-faced woman.

"Nobody is too dinky to have sorrow," said the old woman softly to herself, "an' even the Small People must have their little sorrows, I s'pose."

"You have got the second sight," cried Skerry-Werry, "and you have seen more than your grandmother ever saw!"

"How do you know what my ould grannie saw or did not see?" asked Nance, gazing at the child. "You're only a croom of a cheeld, or look like one, but you do talk like an ancient woman. You be'nt one of the Little Ancients, be 'ee, Skerry-Werry?"

"Why, Mammie Pencarrow, what will you say next?" laughed the child. "Shall we go into the cottage?"

"If you please," murmured the old woman.

Into the little dwelling they went, taking their places by the fire which was blazing on the hearthstone and sending a warm glow over the room.

"Won't you mammie me and call me pretty names like you did the first night I came?" asked the child.

Nance smiled. "I love to mammie you and say pretty things to you." Stooping down, she lifted the child on her lap, but the tiny maid was so heavy it nearly broke Nance's back.

"What a terrible weight you be," she groaned. "I don't

51

believe I shall be able to hold 'ee on my lap more than a minute. The weight of 'ee is breaking my poor ould knees. 'Tis fine an' queer that a little bit of a cheeld like you should be so heavy. You be getting smaller as you be getting heavier. I can't understand it. There! my ould knees have given out already, iss fy, they have!"

As Nance spoke, Skerry-Werry slipped from her knees and fell face down on the cat, who looked as flat as a baking iron when the dinky maid picked herself up.

"I hope I did not hurt you, Tommie Cat," she whispered, patting him, "but I can't have hurt you so much as it hurts me to know that Mammie Pencarrow can no longer hold me on her lap and mammie me."

"I can mammie you in everything else," said Nance stoutly. "Sit on your cricket now an' warm your toes by the fire before we go to bed."

The child seated herself on the stool and sat gazing into the fire, her tiny white face resting on her hands. Her hair, which looked wind-blown even indoors, was a cloud of gold above her brow. The old woman sat and watched her. The cat, who had quickly recovered being fallen upon, got up and sat at his mistress' feet, but he did not purr.

Nance and Skerry-Werry were silent a long time, and everything was very still in the cottage and out. The fire blazed brighter and brighter, its shine and the shadows playing on the white-washed walls. Suddenly the silence was broken by a sad voice crying outside.

"I have lost my little cheeld-whidden. Ah me, what shall I do?"

The old woman started but said never a word. The cat looked toward the door. The child did not move.

In a little while the silence was again broken by the small, sad voice. "I have lost my little cheeld-whidden. Ah me, what shall I do?"

The old woman clutched the elbows of her chair. The cat turned his face to the door. The child sat still, gazing into the fire.

Suddenly Skerry-Werry looked up and said, "Whoever was that crying outside the door?"

"I don't know, my dear, unless it was a nighthawk," returned the old woman.

"I thought a nighthawk's note was a *churrrr,* and now and again a *wh-ip, wh-ip,*" said the child. "The voice I heard outside the door was not like a nighthawk's."

"Perhaps it was a moorhen calling her children to her," said the old woman.

"Perhaps it was," said the child, "but I thought a moorhen's call was *krek-rerk-rerk.* The voice outside the door did not cry *krek-rerk-rerk.*"

"Maybe it was a quail," said the old woman. "His voice is almost as sweet as a flute."

"I know it is," said the child, "for I have heard him often. But, all the same, it is not half so sweet as the voice I heard crying outside the door."

"Perhaps it was a horny-wink," said the old woman.

"I think it could not have been a horny-wink," said the child, "for a horny-wink cries *pet-wit, pet-wit.*"

"It might have been a moor owl we heard."

"The moor owl's flight is soft and silent, but his cry is a scream."

"Perhaps it was a great black raven we heard," said the old woman, "as he was flying across the moors to his home on the cliffs."

"Perhaps it was," said the child, "but I thought a raven's voice was hoarse and loud, and that he called *cawk, cawk.* The voice I heard outside the door was crying as if it had *lost* something."

"Then it must have been a poor mother cow crying out for her baby calf," said the old woman.

"The cow mother says *moo-moo-moo,* and the voice we heard was not crying like that. But perhaps we shall hear the voice again, Mammie Pencarrow."

"I hope not," said the old woman, "for it do hurt like pain."

"Did I hurt you like pain when I cried and said I had no mammie to mammie me?" asked the child.

54

"No fy, you didn't. I wanted only to find the little mammieless thing."

"Did you?" said the child, gazing up into Nance's face, which was looking troubled.

As she was gazing at the old woman, the sad voice was heard again outside the door. "I have lost my little cheeld-whidden. Ah me, what shall I do?"

"It is surely a shorn lamb shivering on the moor, bleating an' crying for its warm soft fleece," said the old woman loud and quickly as if she wanted to drown the voice outside her door.

"I thought a shorn lamb said *baa, baa, b-a-a*," said the child. "The voice we heard did not say *baa, b-a-a*."

"It must have been a mare whinnying for its foal," said the old woman louder and quicker than before.

"The voice I heard did not whinny," said the child.

"Then what did it say?" cried the old woman.

"I want you to tell me."

"P'raps it was the cry of a hare caught in the cruel teeth of a gin," said the old woman.

"If you thought that, you would go out in the dark and set the poor hare free," said the child.

"P'raps it's your own mammie come back to mammie you," said the old woman, and her voice was almost as full of sadness as the little voice she had heard outside.

"Look and see," said the child.

55

Nance turned her face toward the door. There, standing on the drexel, was a beautiful little lady, the same little lady she had seen sitting in the golden carriage drawn by the twelve white horses. As she looked at her, the teeny tiny person lifted up her voice and wrung her hands, "Ah me, I have lost my little cheeld-whidden, what shall I do?" Her voice, pathetic in its woe yet sweeter than music, went straight to Nance's heart.

"If you be her little cheeld-whidden—an' I believe you be," she said, turning to the child, "why don't you run to her? She have got the greater right to you, my little Skerry-Werry," Nance added with a sob in her voice.

"I am her little cheeld-whidden," said the child, "and now that I am too heavy for you to hold on your lap I will go to her to mammie me."

Skerry-Werry got up from the cricket and went toward the door, and as she went she grew visibly smaller. By the time she had reached the little lady standing on the drexel she was only daisy high.

"My little cheeld, my own dear teeny tiny skilly-widden," cried the yearning voice of the mother. "I have found you at last."

The gladness in her voice filled Nance's heart with gladness, and Tommie Cat purred as he had never purred before.

56

SKERRY-WERRY

"I must have mammied a Little Body's cheeld," said the old woman softly. "I'm fine an' glad she has got her own dinky mammie instead of me but, oh dear, oh dear, whatever shall I do without my little Skerry-Werry?

Nance Pencarrow and Tommie Cat went to the door and looked out into the night. At first they saw nothing save the dark and the soft shining of stars. Then, out of the darkness, came the sound of silvery voices and happy laughter. As the old woman looked toward the sound, she saw that the darkness was lit up with a pale green light. Sitting on the turf were hundreds and hundreds of Small People and there in the center, dancing like a butterfly, was her Skerry-Werry!

Piskeys on the Mare's Neck

JOSEY TREGASKIS WAS a small farmer living in the granite district of North Cornwall, and his farm was reclaimed from the moors that surrounded it. He was a hardworking man and simple as a child. Like a child, he loved the stories the moor people told him about the Piskeys who, they said, lived out on Rough Tor and Brown Willy and many another rock-crowned hill in the wild neighborhood.

The same people also told him that the Piskeys came out of the tors in the night and galloped their little bits of ponies over the moors, holding teeny tiny lanterns as they galloped. Josey had often seen dinky lights flying over the moors, but the Piskeys themselves he had never seen till one night when he was riding home from Camelford market.

It was the autumn time when he saddled his mare and rode to market. The glory of the moors had departed. The heath was as brown as brown could be, and the grass bunched into tussocks. There was hardly any color to be seen on the moors that day save where the dwarf furze showed gleams of gold, or where a thorn bush was rich in scarlet berries. The only touches of green

59

were tiny paths that led over the moors to the great hills. These were the Piskey roads, and they were bright as the greenest moss.

"Winter will soon be upon us," said Josey Tregaskis as he sent his quick glance over the great open country, "and then the wind and the Small People will have it all their own way."

Camelford market was an important one, and Josey, meeting many friends there, tarried late. It was close on midnight when he got to the moors.

His mare, whose name was Bess, was delighted to find herself on the moors on her homeward way, and she went like the wind on the soft turf. She had been born in the open and had run wild there by her dam's side till she was broken in. The moorland was still her home, and she tossed her rough head and sniffed the night air as she went along. Whenever she passed under a hill, she would prick up her ears and whinny as if she sensed something her master did not.

"What's the matter, old girl?" cried Josey, trying to pierce the darkness that lay upon the moorland. As he looked, he saw scores and scores of tiny lights traveling at a great speed over the turf.

"The Piskeys are galloping their little bits of ponies over the moors, if my eyes don't deceive me," he said aloud to his mare. "I expect you can see the wee chaps on the backs of the Piskey ponies and want to be off after them." He reached over and patted the mare. "I'll keep a strong hand on the rein in case you do."

The mare, with her ears still on the prick, kept up her quick gallop until she came to one of the middle moors, then she went slower. As she was passing a great furze brake, she whinnied again and arched her neck. The next moment the farmer saw the amazing sight of two dinky men on the crest of her neck and one astride her left ear! They were ever so small, not much bigger than a man's thumb. The one on the mare's ear held a lantern about the size of a lark's egg, and from it came a wonderful light, strong enough to show the dinky men clearly.

Josey was too astonished even to utter an exclamation. He sat in his saddle, staring with open mouth at the odd-looking fellows, who took scant notice of him. They were brown-faced, much-whiskered little men, dressed as he had always heard Piskeys described, in red pointed caps, green coats, and dark breeches. They looked exceedingly old and had an artful expression in their dark mysterious eyes, and their brown hands were the hands of very aged men.

Josey did not like their looks at all and longed to flip them off the mare's head with his whip, but he dared not do this. He wondered whether Bess knew that the

61

Piskeys were on her head, and he came to the conclusion that she did, for every now and then she made funny little sounds as mares sometimes do when they talk to their colts. But she went on at a steady trot all the same.

They were halfway over the great moor when the three little men began to talk and laugh, but the farmer could not understand a word they were saying. The only words that sounded Cornish to his ears were the "Hah, hah, hahs" and the "Hee, hee, haws!"

When they grew tired of laughing and talking, the two imps on the mare's head threaded their little brown fingers through her mane, and the other small fellow tickled her ear with his scrap of a finger. He looked so ridiculously funny as he tickled it that Josey would have laughed out loud if he had not been so scared.

"I wish I was safe in my own house," said Farmer Tregaskis to himself as he kept his eyes on the dinky men. "I only hope those queer little chaps aren't preparing some surprise for me. Perhaps they want to drive me and the mare into one of the Piskey bogs and keep us there till I'm old and gray."

The dinky man tickling Bess's ear looked up at Josey and winked as much as to say, "It would be a splendid joke if we did."

Bess, with the little men on her neck and ear, cantered on and never heeded them save to give voice to her pleasure in the way that we have said. Lights from Piskey lanterns ran along the turf and Josey Tregaskis, as he watched them, knew that many Piskeys were out riding their ponies on the moors and letting their lanterns flash as they rode.

The fairy lights and the stars shining above the big rocky hills were the only brightness visible on the far-reaching moor save for the light from the tiny lantern which the dinky man held in one hand as he tickled the mare's head with the other. This shed a warm glow over himself and his elf companions and the rough head of the mare.

Bess went on and on to the farmer's thankfulness in the direction of home.

After riding many miles, Josey heard the friendly bark of a sheep dog in the distance. As the bark came up sharp and clear over the moor, the light from the dinky man's lantern went suddenly out. But Josey knew that the three of them were still on the head of the mare for he could hear their laughing and talking. Their queer voices did not cease till Bess stopped at the farmhouse gate. A strange silence followed and then, after a minute or less, a "Hah, hah, hee!" on the edge of the moor close to the farm.

Farmer Tregaskis led his mare to her stable. When he

had lighted the horn lantern that hung over her stall, he saw that her mane was plaited into little tails and that some of them were looped into stirrups and others woven into panniers.

"Well, I never did," cried the farmer when he saw what the dinky men had done. "I thought they were up to something. 'Tis plain as a moor cross that the whole tribe of Piskey men meant to have a ride on old Bess over the moors tonight for here are scores of stirrups and panniers ready for them to stand on and sit in."

While he took off the saddle and rubbed the mare's back with straw, Josey went on talking to himself. "I wonder what prevented them from carrying out their intention," he said. "Me, perhaps, for I am certain sure that the little rascal who tickled the mare's ear did it on purpose to make her as mad as a curley and to pitch me off. He tickled her enough to pitch off the best rider that ever rode a skittish mare like Bess." Farmer Tregaskis wagged his head and gave Bess a pat.

"But she was true to her master," he went on, "and she shall have a good feed of corn on the strength of it. Then I'll lock her safe in her stable and take the key to bed with me. The Piskeys can't take her out through the keyhole, that's certain, though I've heard tell they're artful enough to do anything."

64

PISKEYS ON THE MARE'S NECK

So Josey bedded the mare down and gave her a good measure of corn, and Bess repaid him with a whinny that said far more than the little sounds she had made to the Piskeys riding between her ears.

The Piskey
Warriors

IF THERE IS a moor more full of legendary tales than another, it is the Goss Moor. The old people brought up on it used to tell many a weird legend about the wild, lonely spot. One of these was a woman called Emlyn Moyle; a charming old body with shining seer's eyes, gray like her own carns, and soft hair white and silky like Piskey wool showing under her clean, starched cap.

This old woman was born and brought up in a small hamlet named Belovely, or Belowda, which stands right on the moor and consists of a few cottages facing Castle-an-Dinas. Emlyn's cottage was one of the oldest in the village. It was thatched and whitewashed and under the thatch peeped tiny casement windows.

Emlyn was a born story teller like the old people before her, and many a tale she told to her friends. Sometimes, she told them on winter evenings as they sat around the peat fire while the fierce wind swept by their village; sometimes, in the spring when she and other neighbors were on the moor looking after their geese, for most of the women of Belovely kept geese. The great moor was dotted with their geese huts, little shelters made of earth and stone, their turfen roofs often white

67

with daisies or golden with trefoils. In these huts the geese would lay their eggs and hatch out their young.

Emlyn was never happier than when telling tales of the Piskeys and other Small People. When she was young, the men and maids of Belovely used to go out on the moor to hunt for fairies who knew where gold was hidden. For it was believed that the Little People were the keepers of the treasure buried in some forgotten time, perhaps by a different race of men from those now living on the moor. Emlyn told her listeners where the Piskeys were said to dwell, of their little walks—tiny paths of brightest green—where they took their strolls when the evening star came up behind the hills.

She told of little men who rode the Goss Moor ponies when the moon was high, and how they were all booted and spurred and clad in white breeches, red riding coats, and soft hats, and how they rode till the sun began to rise behind the eastern range of hills. She told them, too, a weird tale about Giant Tregeagle who, when a storm raged over the moor, flew by like the wind to Roche Rocks. A little hermitage stood there, dedicated to St. Michael.

"Old Tregeagle would tear along with the Bad One behind him," Emlyn said, "knowing that if only he could thrust his head inside that sanctuary he would be safe."

But the tales she liked best to tell were about Castle-

68

an-Dinas, the large, entrenched camp standing some seven hundred feet above the sea. Some said it was British, some Danish, with its three great rings, or vallums, on its brow built of turf and unwrought stone.

According to the old people who lived at Belovely when Emlyn was a little maid, the Castle had been King Arthur's hunting-seat. One day, it was said, when hunting the wild boar, King Arthur's horse stamped hard on a moorstone and left the prints of his hoofs upon it. The hoofprints are still on the stone to show the natives of the moorland that in the long ago Arthur and his knights came and stayed at Castle-an-Dinas and went riding on their own moor.

Another tale Emlyn used to tell was of a great battle fought hundreds of years ago somewhere on the moor, perhaps on Castle-an-Dinas itself. Whether one really had been fought or not, nobody could ever say, but the legend has it that, when the mists cover the hills and the moor, little Piskey warriors, tiny men in scarlet jackets, refight that battle on the outer circle of the great entrenched hill, perhaps where it was first fought. People passing near the Castle in the fog have heard their battle cries and the crashing of tiny arms. Stopping to listen, they would whisper to each other, "The little bits of men are fighting that great battle over again."

This strange legend may be a fragment of some forgotten tale of an invading race, perhaps the Danish, which fought to get possession of the land. It may speak of that weird conflict in the west when King Arthur and his hosts fought their last great fight—

"And ever pushed Sir Modred league by league
Back to the sunset bounds of Lyonesse."

As they fought and drove the rebels down to where the sunset fires the cliffs, the mists closed in upon them, taking strange shapes of beasts and men that were not men. This chilled their hearts and brains till they knew not friend from foe, and friends slew friends not knowing what they did.

Whether there was any truth at all in the wild tale of a battle, handed down from a dim past by the natives of the moor, Emlyn could not say. However, when the old camp has been shut in by thick mist, many have heard the warriors fighting their mimic fight, and some have seen them when the fog has lifted for a moment. Emlyn was one of those who both heard and saw.

It happened in this way.

One day when the orchises were sending up their pale green spikes to break into purple flower and the broom was glowing with golden blossom, Emlyn went to tend her geese, who were hatching out their young. The air was full of the fragrance of wild flowers blossoming near

70

the pools scattered over the great moor. The heather was still brown under the April sky, but it was washed with silver sunlight here and there.

The birds were full of high intent, bringing food to their families hidden in the furze brakes. Larks were singing above, pouring their wealth of rapturous song on their little brown mates sitting on tiny, freckled eggs on the turfen sods. The day was clear as well as mild, and the distant hills were blue as air. Castle-an-Dinas with its triple rings stood out plainly against a background of sky.

" 'Tis a day to make your heart sing as well as the birds," Emlyn said to herself as she took her seat near the geese huts.

There the gray, patient geese were sitting, watched over by Father Gander, who shot out his long white neck snakewise and hissed his disapproval. But Emlyn heeded him not and took out her knitting, looking about her as she did so. There was much to see. Not far away were pools where flocks of geese and goslings sailed over the surface of the clear brown water, each a boat of gray or gold. The willows surrounding the pools were golden, too, with yellow catkins, or goose-chicks as the natives called them because they were round and soft like goslings.

In the course of the morning, one of Emlyn's geese

71

hatched out several of her chicks. Emlyn took them from the mother and wrapped them in flannel till the rest were hatched. If she had not, the silly goose would have waddled off with her little chicks of fluffy gold and left the ones unhatched to die of cold within the eggs. Such is the way of geese when they are left unwatched.

As the morning drew toward noon, the character of the moor began to change. Emlyn, as she sat with the goose-chicks in her lap, saw a thin cloud of mist steal over the head of Castle-an-Dinas.

"There is a fog coming up over the Castle," she said to herself. "I hope it won't spread and thicken till the old goose has hatched out the rest of her chicks."

The goose was not so obliging as Emlyn had hoped, and the mist had crept over all the hills near and far and half-hidden the moor before she left the turfen shelter with the last of her hatched goslings.

Emlyn had no sooner set the flannel-wrapped goslings free when the goose and all her little brood went off to the nearest pool. They were accompanied by Father Gander, who gave vent to his feelings in loud shrill cries as he proudly led his family to the water by the sallows. Emlyn went after them to bring them back, and, by the time she had done this and fed them, the fog had shut out everything from view.

"I hope I shan't lose my way going home," she said as

72

she started for Belovely. "It is thick as a hedge already, and I can't see the length of my hand."

She felt her way along. After she had been walking some time, she put her foot into a hole and fell. She was unhurt, but she felt bewildered, like one Piskey-ridden, and went on her way hardly knowing where she was going. She went down and up, but could not find her way. Suddenly her steps were arrested by strange little cries coming out of the mist and the sound of clashing; what it was she did not know. Then, with a flash, came back the legend of the old battle and the Piskey warriors fighting the mimic fight in the mist on the outer ring of the Castle.

"Wherever have I got to?" she muttered as the cries came louder through the thick fog. "I can never be up on the Castle! But if I have wandered up here in the mist, I must be close to the outside ring." She bent her head to listen. "I can hear the little warriors quite near, and they're fighting like dragons. I can hear the sounds of their little swords. Oh, I do hope I shan't see them, too!"

Emlyn had scarcely said this when the fog parted in front of her, and through the rift she saw the top of the Castle and its three entrenchments. Not far away were hundreds of little men in red jackets in battle order. In their tiny hands were tiny swords.

PIXIE FOLKLORE

It was a dreadful battle the Piskey warriors were fighting not many yards from where the old woman stood. They were terribly in earnest, and they looked so fierce, so strange and old—thousands of years old, perhaps. Emlyn longed to turn and fly, but she dared not move for fear of drawing attention to herself. So she stood still, watching the mimic battle fought by little men. How long she stood on the circle she never could tell, she knew only that it seemed hours and hours.

Time and again she saw them rush at each other, uttering their battle cries, striking at each other with their little swords. The mist curled in between them as they thrust and parried. Then, when Emlyn felt she could not watch another moment, the fog met again and made a wall between her and the little warriors, hiding them from her sight. But the battle was evidently to be fought to a finish, and their weird cries and the noise of sword striking sword still came through the mist.

Emlyn did not move for the fog was thick around her, and she kept quite still till the sounds had ceased. Hardly had they ceased when the fog lifted and over the Castle the moon shone white and clear. On the circle, where she had almost dreaded to see slain bodies of little warriors still grasping elfin swords, she saw nothing but sleeping flowers. There was not a sign anywhere that a battle had been fought.

74

"I s'pose I did see the Piskey warriors fighting, as others have seen them before me," Emlyn said to herself as she went on her way to Belovely. "If I did, I don't ever want to see them fighting again, not even if they were only playing at fighting that great battle fought hundreds and hundreds of years ago."

Such was the weird tale old Emlyn told of the mimic battle fought on the outer circle of Castle-an-Dinas which the natives of the moor still say was King Arthur's hunting-seat.

The Nurse Who Broke Her Promise

IN A FARAWAY time there lived in one of the wildest and remotest of Cornish parishes an old nurse. The name of this nurse was Alsey Trenowth, and whenever a little child was expected Alsey was sent for.

One day a mysterious message came for her to go to a place she had never heard of before, and because the message was urgent she put on her cloak and her hood and went.

When the old nurse got to the place, she was bewildered, for it was the most outlandish place she had ever seen in her life, and the tiny house dug out of the side of a cliff was the only dwelling in sight. There was nothing to be seen for miles and miles but lonely downs with a background of great hills, each with a burthen of granite boulders. The only sounds that broke the silence were the cries of peewits, the wild sweet song of birds, the ripple of water flowing out of the bogs near the tors, and the wind singing through the flowering furze and greening sallows.

"Wherever in the world have I got to?" said Alsey to herself as she gazed about. "I never saw such a queer place in all my born days, and I have been to many queer places in my time. This dinky house is like a Piskey dwelling, iss fy, it is! I don't know how I got here. I must have been Piskey-led indeed." She sighed heavily, "I wish I hadn't come, but having come I s'pose I can't turn back home till I see what's wanted of me."

She entered the hut as she spoke. It consisted of one low room whose rugged walls were formed by the sides of the cliff. In a corner on a heap of bracken lay a tiny brown woman with very dark eyes. The tiny person said not a word, but her gaze never left Alsey's face.

"The little brown woman looks as outlandish as the place," muttered the nurse to herself. "I wish she wouldn't stare at me so. 'Tis as if she wants to read my thoughts or look into my soul."

In due time the child arrived, and Alsey was glad to see it, for the tiny stranger seemed to make the lonely place less lonely. It was a brown babe, almost as brown as its odd-looking mother, and the smallest babe Alsey had ever seen.

"It cannot be much bigger than a Piskey's cheeld," she said to herself as she gazed at it "It is like a skilly-widden."

When the nurse wanted to give the babe a bath, she looked around to see if there was anything to wash it in, and as she looked she saw, to her astonishment, a tiny man standing near the door watching her. He had long hair and a very long beard, and his skin was dark of hue like that of the dinky woman on the bracken. He was dressed in gray breeches and stockings and brown, pointed shoes. On his head he wore a green steeple hat, and over his shoulders was flung a bright red cloak.

Alsey almost jumped out of her skin with fright when she saw such an odd-looking little man gazing at her; and she almost dropped the babe.

"I did not know you were here," she cried as soon as she could find her tongue. "You startled me so that you could have knocked me down with a feather."

"Could I?" said he with a laugh. "You might have seen me before if you had only used your eyes. I have been in the room ever since you have been in it."

"Have you?" said Alsey, not knowing what else to say, he made her feel so uncomfortable.

"Yes," responded the dinky man. "The woman over there lying in the corner is my wife, and that little skilly-widden on your arm is my son, of whom I am very proud."

"Are you?" said the nurse, glancing down on the brown little babe. "Well, I want to give him a bath if I can find anything in this outlandish place to do it in."

"There is a basin behind the door," said the brown man, and Alsey, looking, saw a vessel full of very clear water. As she was about to put the babe into it, the brown man said, "I beg you to be very careful in washing my skillywidden and not let any of the water splash into your eyes."

"I'll be careful," laughed the nurse, "but you shouldn't teach your grannie to rake ashes. This is not the first newborn babe I have washed by many, let me tell you."

"I know it isn't," said the tiny man, "or you would not have been sent for to wash my skillywidden, but I advise you, all the same, not to let the water you wash him in touch your eyes."

"Why not?" asked Alsey, who was getting over her fear of the brown man. "Would it hurt my eyes if I did?"

"I want you to promise not to wash in that water after you have washed my skillywidden," repeated the man.

"I am not likely to do anything so foolish," said the old nurse with a toss of her white-capped head.

"But I want you to promise you will do nothing so foolish."

"Then I promise," said the old woman lightly.

"Good!" cried the brown man. "But remember, if you break your promise you will be sorry for it." His dark searching eyes seemed to look her through and through as he spoke, then he turned and left the hut.

"The folks in this outlandish place have got eyes like needles," muttered Alsey. "Even this dinky babe seems to have the power to pierce me through as I wash him."

When the old nurse had washed the skillywidden and given him to his mother, she took up the basin to throw away the water, which was still clear and full of light and sparkle.

"It's the brightest water I ever saw," she said as she looked at it. "It is so clear and sparkling that it might have come out of a Piskey's well. I wonder if that's the reason the little brown man did not want me to wash my eyes in it. I can't for the life of me see why I shouldn't." She stood gazing into the basin for ever so long.

There was no sound in the hut save the soft murmur of a voice in the far corner of the room as the little brown woman talked to her babe. The longer the old nurse stood looking into the water, the more she wanted to do what she had promised not to do. Every sparkle in the water seemed to tempt her to wash her eyes in it.

"Such beautiful water cannot possibly harm me," she said to herself. "Indeed, it was more than foolish of me to promise that odd little man not to wash my eyes in it. A bad promise like a bad egg is better broken than kept, I'm thinking, and I don't see why I can't break mine.

"Besides," she went on, "I want to know what will happen to me if I do wash my eyes in this water. Nothing dreadful, I daresay, after coming to this out-of-the-way spot to do a kindness to a stranger."

81

She turned her glance to where the brown woman was cooing to her skillywidden, then she looked back at the water. "Come ill, come well, I'll take my chance!" she cried.

Fearing her courage would fail if she hesitated any longer, Alsey washed her eyes in the water quickly and then, half afraid but wholly curious, opened them and glanced around her.

To her astonishment the hut looked entirely different. It was no longer rough, poor, and mean but bright and beautiful as a Piskey palace and full of Little People. They were beautiful Little People, too, and so were the garments they wore which outvied the moorland flowers in color and brightness.

The tiny folk were amusing themselves variously. Some were talking and laughing, some were singing, others were playing and dancing. Several little ladies were sitting on the bed, which was now formed of flowers instead of bracken, chirping to the skillywidden. The babe did not even look like the babe Alsey had just washed but like the prettiest little thing imaginable. "As sweet as mayflowers," said Alsey to herself.

The old nurse was frightened now, as well as astonished, for she knew that by the breaking of a promise she had obtained the faculty, not only of seeing the Small

People, but of hearing them too. She felt far from happy as she stood gazing on the amazing scene.

The Piskeys were apparently unconscious that Alsey could see them and took no more notice of her than they would of a stick. They talked and laughed, danced, played and sang as if she was not present. The tiny ladies sitting on the bed clucked and cooed to the newly born as if the old nurse had not been looking on.

"The babe I washed was a Piskey's babe," said Alsey to herself, "and the water I washed him in was fairy water, I'm certain sure. How foolish I was to wash my eyes in it! I'm sorry already that I broke my promise, for I'm afraid to stay any longer in a house full of Piskeys."

She put the basin gently on the floor and stole quietly away, followed by the laughter of tiny voices.

Alsey made her way back as best she could to the village where she lived, but how she got back she never could tell. She knew only that she was long in getting there and that, wherever she turned her gaze, she saw the Small People. They sat on Piskey stools on the downs as if they were sitting there to enjoy the view. Where the turf was green and sweet with thyme, they danced to the strains of pipes and fiddles. Not far from where the dancing was going on, Alsey met a colt with night-riders on his back. They rode for all they were worth over the downs. Little scamps they were and little

83

scamps they looked in their riding coats, boots, and breeches and soft slouch hats in each of which was stuck a tiny feather. They made long noses at poor, frightened Alsey as they galloped past her on the still more frightened colt.

Where the tableland sloped to the marshes and the sea, she saw hobgoblins, which made her wish more than ever that she had never been sent for to welcome a Piskey's babe. "For then," she moaned, "I should never have been tempted. Oh, if only I had not broken my promise," she cried as the hobgoblins gazed at her with great protruding eyes.

Thankful beyond measure was poor Alsey when she found herself at last within the shelter of her own neat cottage, close to human sights and sounds. But even there she could not put from her the dearly bought new sight, for elves peeped at her through her window, laughed and talked outside her door. Even in her bed-chamber she was not free from the Small People, for many a laughing face looked down at her from the bed-tester as she lay in bed.

"My little home and all the parish is haunted by Piskeys," she said, "and I never knew it till I was foolish enough to wash my eyes in the water in which I washed a brown man's skillywidden."

A few days later Alsey had occasion to go to the market town. It was several miles away from her own village, and, as she was afraid to be out after dark now she had the faculty of seeing the Little People, she set out soon after sunrise.

The way to the town led through moors where asphodels made golden light and buckbeans sent up silver spires, through ferny lanes sweet with many a blossom where finches sang and blackbirds made musical conversations. On the moors and in the lanes, Alsey saw Piskeys peeping at her from shining beds of asphodels, from purple patches of heather, from flower-smothered hedges. Little red-capped, green-coated elves eyed her curiously as they swung from long-stalked foxgloves that made the high Cornish lanes very beautiful.

When she reached the market town, people from all the country round were pouring into it. The market place was full of stalls as well as people, and when the old nurse could get near the stalls, from which almost anything might be bought, whom should she see but the little brown man who had made her promise not to wash her eyes in the water in which she had washed his babe.

The old woman recognized him at once by his long hair and beard and his gay dress; but she was so surprised to see him in a public market that she could only stand still and look as he moved in and out among the stalls and the people. What surprised her still more was that nobody, not even the stallkeepers, took any notice of the scarlet-cloaked little person in the steeple-crowned hat. She came to the conclusion that he must be as invisible to their eyes as he was visible to hers.

Alsey watched him for ever so long, and, when he came near enough for her to see what he was doing, she was shocked to find that he was helping himself from every stall he stopped at, hiding stolen goods under his scarlet cloak.

"That little brown man is a thief," said the old nurse to herself as she watched him. "Humph, that's the reason, is it, he didn't want me to wash my eyes in that water, for fear I should spy upon him robbing poor folks' stalls! Bad luck to him. What a hullabaloo there would be if the stallkeepers knew how they were being robbed by a Piskey!"

She made her way to a stall laden with eatables where the brown man was stuffing himself with good things; all at the expense of the stallkeeper, who apparently did not see the Piskey sitting right under his nose and helping himself to the dainties so temptingly laid out.

The astonishing discovery that the little man was a thief took away Alsey's fear of him. She went up to him quite boldly, holding out her hand. "Good morrow to 'ee, my dear," she said in her homely Cornish fashion, "and how be you?"

NURSE WHO BROKE HER PROMISE

It was now the little brown man's turn to be astonished. "I did not know that you could see *me*," he cried, looking up at her from under his steeple-crowned hat. "I saw you here, of course, and recognized you when you came into the market as the old body who welcomed the arrival of my little skillywidden."

"Yes, I'm that one, Alsey Trenowth by name," the nurse smiled.

"But I am a Piskey," the little man went on, "and nobody living can have the gift of seeing the Piskeys unless it is given for some unusual kindness to the Small People or obtained by something forbidden. I fear you got your gift by washing your eyes in water in which a skillywidden was washed. Did you?"

"I did," responded the old nurse as the brown man's dark eyes fixed themselves on her.

"Did you?" he cried. "I might have known that a woman of your kidney would break a promise as lightly as she made it."

"I wanted only to see what would happen," said the old woman, feeling both ashamed and unhappy as he looked at her with his searching eyes.

"Which shows that you are but a daughter of Eve," he said contemptuously. "The gift of seeing the Piskeys obtained by the breaking of a promise can bring neither pleasure nor happiness and can be taken back only by

87

one of their tribe. In spite of your kindness to my little wife, I'll take back what you took, and you shall never again be able to see the Small People."

He looked at her long and earnestly then added, "And something which would have been bestowed on you for washing a Piskey's babe will never be yours."

He touched the old nurse's eyes as he spoke, then vanished, and Alsey never saw him or any of the other Little People again. She was not at all sorry she had lost the faculty of seeing the Little People, but she never stopped wondering what that "something" was that would have been hers if she had not broken her promise to a Piskey.

The Curious Woman of Davidstow

IN THE PARISH of Davidstow lived a woman called Lucy. She lived all by herself in a small stone-porched cottage on one of the moors. She was a very nice woman, honest and clean, and she kept her little home spotless.

She was as healthy and strong as people who live in the fresh moorland air ought to be, but it fell out one year that she became ill and weak. Consequently, she was no longer able to keep her cottage tidy.

This was a sore trouble to one so cleanly as Lucy, and when she saw her little place getting dirtier and dirtier it greatly distressed her. She wished that the Piskeys would come and clean it for her now she was not able to do it herself.

There were Piskeys living among the carns out on Rough Tor and Brown Willy, and when night came, so the old people of Davidstow said, they would come up over the moors to the cottages and look in at the windows. If they saw that any of the rooms wanted cleaning and there was nobody to clean them, they got in through the keyholes and did all the work. Many stories were told about the Piskeys' kindness in cottage cleaning which came back to Lucy's mind now, and she longed for them to do the same kindness to her.

"But perhaps they don't do it these days," Lucy thought sadly to herself.

All one day she was more troubled than usual about the state of her little home, and when she dragged herself up to her bedchamber at night she could not sleep a wink.

The next morning when she got up and went downstairs the first thing she saw on opening the door of her living room was that somebody had been in and cleaned it up. "It's as fresh as a butter printer just washed and dried," said Lucy, "and smelling as sweet as moor flowers!"

The hearth was swept and the hearthstone washed and the flagged floor too, all looking as blue as the azure hills. Everything was in its place and everything was spotless. Her square oak table and old-fashioned, fiddle-backed chairs were polished and shining, and as for the cloam on the dresser—it looked as if it had just been washed in moorland dew!

Lucy could scarcely believe her eyesight and passed her hand over her eyes to make sure she was not dreaming.

" 'Tis no dream," she cried with a happy laugh as she gazed first at one thing and then at another. "The Piskeys

90

must have come up from Rough Tor and Brown Willy and found out how dirty my little place was, for they it is who've cleaned it for me. I feel better already only to see everything looking so tidy and fresh. I shall be able to sit in my chair in comfort now," she went on, "and enjoy my dish of tea. I do hope they will come again."

The Piskeys did come again, every night for quite a long time, for when Lucy came downstairs in the morning she found everything clean as a new pin. Nothing was left undone that ought to be done.

Lucy was very grateful to the Piskeys for keeping her place so spotless; but, as she grew better in health and became more accustomed to their wonderful kindness, she began to get curious about them and wondered what they were like, and she longed to see them cleaning up her cottage.

So, one lovely night when the moonshine was white on the moors and the distant Tintagel waves, which she could see from her casement window, she heard a noise as if a chair were being moved across the room. She realized that the Little People were downstairs working. Out of bed she got, crept from her small bedchamber and down the narrow stairs. When she reached the door, she put her eye to the keyhole, which was a large wooden one, and peeped in.

The room was full of a soft light—whether moonlight

or Piskey light she could not tell—and the light lit the room and everything in it, including the Piskeys. The room was full of them, little men and women not much bigger than clothes pegs, and they were all as busy as a flock of starlings in a stubble field.

Lucy was delighted to be able to see the Piskeys so hard at work, and the businesslike way in which they were doing their work made her almost laugh out loud. The tiny women Piskeys had the skirts of their bright little gowns pinned up around them like careful house-wives, and the little men had their coat sleeves turned up to the elbow.

Lucy was amazed how such dinky folk could manage to do the work they did, and so well too. Two little men Piskeys were up on the back of one of her chairs rubbing away as hard as they could rub and laughing as they rubbed. Two more were on the seat also rubbing, and two were on the floor rubbing the legs.

"Six to a chair," said Lucy to herself.

Then she looked up at the dresser, which was full of china both coarse and fine. The Piskeys were there like a swarm of bees. There seemed to be as many Piskeys as there were cups and saucers, plates and jugs. One of the little, wizened men was astride the handle of a big Toby jug, and Lucy nearly laughed out loud again because he looked so funny, especially when he winked his eye at one of the little women Piskeys sitting on a knob of the dresser. Every shelf had at least a dozen dinky men in red coats and pointed hats. Everyone of them was polishing the dresser and the china that filled it, and everyone looked as if work was only play.

"I have heard tell that the Piskeys love work," said Lucy to herself as she watched them, "and now I can believe it."

Next she looked at the tiny women who were also rubbing and dusting, laughing gaily to themselves as they rubbed and dusted. The floor and hearth had evidently been done, and the soft light falling upon them made them look even bluer than the hills.

Lucy remained looking through the keyhole for ten minutes or more, and the longer she looked the longer she wanted to look. The Little People were so fascinating. No one could say how long she would have gone on prying on her friends—for it was prying—if a little Piskey woman had not suddenly turned and looked hard at the keyhole through which Lucy was gazing. This frightened Lucy, and she crept quietly back to her bedchamber.

She was too excited to go to bed again and so sat by the window till the moon set, very red and very large, over the headland of Trevose and the sun came up behind the eastern tors.

The curious woman, having spied on the Piskeys through the keyhole, could not rest, and all that day they were in her thoughts. By evening she wondered if she should not thank them personally for their kindness in keeping her cottage like a new penny. The only way she felt that she could do this was to creep downstairs again when they were working, open the door, and go into the room.

That night she again heard the Piskeys move a chair or table across the room under her chamber. Out of bed she got and stole from her room and down the stairs. Without waiting even to peep through the keyhole to make sure they were there, she put her finger and thumb to the latch, opened the door, and went in.

The room was full of Little People all as busy as on the previous night, but Lucy had only got inside when they vanished.

"My dear life! The Piskeys have everyone o' mun gone!" she cried in dismay. "And I was going to thank them so nicely, too, for keeping my cottage clean and sweet, and now my coming in upon them unexpected-like has frightened them all away. What a pity I didn't let well alone!"

Lucy looked around the room, then she shook her head sadly, "I'm afraid they will never come and clean up my place any more, and what I shall do I don't know."

94

CURIOUS WOMAN OF DAVIDSTOW

Lucy was quite right. The Piskeys never came near her again. And for some time after she had bounced in on them, she had to live in a dirty cottage until she was well enough to clean it herself.

Why Jan Pendogget Changed His Mind

JAN PENDOGGET WAS a very obstinate person, especially in the matter of the Little People. He said there were no such beings, *not even Piskeys,* whom everybody in Cornwall believed in except himself. His mother could not understand such unbelief and told Jan the Piskeys would serve him out for it one of these odd days as sure as his name was Pendogget.

Jan was really a very nice man and good to his old mother, who kept house for him. He was the owner of a few acres of land and, like most farmers in his part of the world, went to all the markets and fairs near enough to be got at; partly to sell his bullocks and pigs and partly to hear the gossip and crack jokes with his fellow farmers.

One day, when he was getting ready to go to Summer Court Fair, his mother remarked that the Piskeys were making their rings in Undertown, a large meadow which Jan would have to cross on his return to the house.

"Well, what of that?" he asked teasingly. "Do 'ee think the Piskeys are setting traps for me?"

"You may laugh, Jan, my son," returned Mrs. Pen-

PIXIE FOLKLORE

dogget with a shake of her head, "but I have noticed times without number that whenever the Piskeys make rings they have their jokes upon somebody. So I warn 'ee to be careful you don't tread on the Piskey rings in coming home through the field. You will be Piskey-led as sure as fate if you do."

Jan, who was like a giant in both size and strength, chaffered his mother for her silly nonsense and said that even if there were such creatures as Piskeys they would have a hard job to Piskey-lead him! Then, chuckling to himself, he went away to the fair.

Jan left Summer Court Fair quite early in the evening. Very pleased he was with himself for he had made a good sale of his pigs and had bought a fairing for his mother in the shape of a bright red ribbon for her jinny-quick cap. Being the end of September, the days were closing in early, and by the time Jan had crossed the moors and reached Undertown it was as dark as a sack.

Undertown meadow had two gates, one leading out on to the moors and the other in to the townplace, or farm yard, of Jan's farm. Jan found the first gate quite easily. When he had closed it behind him he remembered what his mother had said about the Piskeys making their rings in the meadow. He laughed aloud as he thought of it and of his mother's warning.

His laugh was taken up by somebody on the other side

of the hedge. This vexed Jan so that he called out and said he would give whoever it was "what for" when he got hold of him. Thinking it was one of his own men, he strode up the great meadow in anger.

When he reached the end of the meadow and felt for the gate leading in to the townplace, he could not find it. This surprised him, for he knew the bearings of the meadow better than he knew his mother's face. When he went round the hedge surrounding the field and could find neither gate, his surprise gave place to amazement. Not liking to be done, he went round and round the meadow until his patience was exhausted.

"Drat it all," he cried, "whatever has come over me?"

As he voiced his feelings, a peal of laughter broke upon the night. This made Jan very angry, and once more he made frantic efforts to find the gates; but the more he tried the more confused he became and the louder grew the laughter.

"Dang it," he exclaimed, shaking his fists at his invisible tormentors. "They ought to be ashamed of themselves whoever they be. I'll be even with 'em yet if they come anist me."

Whoever they were, they only laughed louder and more tantalizingly than before until Jan stamped his feet with fury. Once more his big voice, threatening all manner of vengeance, roared out into the darkness.

99

Finding he could not put his hand on the gates, Jan strode across the meadow. As he was going he saw hundreds of tiny lights in the grass.

"Glowworms," he cried, "I'll get a few of them. They'll light me to the gate," and the great fellow dropped on all fours to the ground, stretching out his big paw to lay hold of the yellow lights flashing up from the grass.

The glowworms, as he thought they were, were not so easily caught, for the moment his hand descended on a tiny flame—it was burning yards ahead of him!

"I am bewitched," he said at last, "or glowworms are more difficult to catch than seahoppers."

He got up and gazed at the soft twinkling lights mournfully, then he noticed that they were arranging themselves round a space of the meadow where he was standing. When they had formed into a large ring, the lights began to bob up and down like a jack-o'-lantern and to twirl and untwirl in a kind of fire dance. Each movement was followed by peals of mirthful laughter, and Jan felt queer and afraid for the first time since he was breeched.

"They must be Piskey lights," said the farmer, rubbing his head ruefully, reluctant to admit, even to himself, the possibility of such things and the evidence of his own eyes, "and I must have stepped into a Piskey ring!"

WHY JAN CHANGED HIS MIND

Jan Pendogget was in the habit of thinking his thoughts aloud, and the Piskeys who were holding him prisoner laughed at the admission he had made. The laughter was so good natured and so infectious that Jan soon was laughing too.

"I know now what 'laughing like a Piskey' means," he said, wiping his eyes with the sleeve of his coat, "an' 'tis good to laugh like that sometimes, I reckon. But, dear little chaps," he pleaded, looking down at the twinkling lights, "I know now for sure and certain that there *are* Piskeys, and since you have had the laughing side of me, please let me go home to my mother. She'll be fretting herself blue not knowing what is keeping me."

No answer came from the ring of lights so Jan tried again.

"She's a good sort, as p'raps you know, and believes in the whole lot of 'ee. She thinks the world of you Piskeys, she do indeed. Do 'ee take this bewitchment or whatever it is off me, that's kind little chaps, and show me the whereabouts of my gate. If you will, little sirs, I'll never say an unkind word about 'ee, never no more, and I'll believe in 'ee with all my parts."

Jan said all this in his most wheedling voice, the voice he used when he wanted to get over his mother, but he might just as well have held his tongue for all the notice the Piskeys took of him.

PIXIE FOLKLORE

The dancing and the laughter went on for hours in the pitchy darkness and Jan, poor fellow, six feet two in his stockings and broad in proportion, was compelled to stand in the center of the ring, held by the Piskey spell which he could not break. The frolic became more furious as time went by and the laughter louder, while the Piskey lights flashed so constantly that Jan's eyes became dazed and his head giddy.

Just before the breaking of the day, Jan remembered a story which his mother had told him of a Piskey-led man and of how he had found his way out of a field by turning his coat inside out.

"What a sheep's-head I am!" he cried, "not to have remembered it before! That chap had off with his jacket in a trice and put it on outside in, and so will I."

In a winky Jan's best go-a-fair coat was off his back and turned. In another winky it was on again and the spell was broken. The Piskeys and their dazzling lights vanished and the long-held prisoner found himself making for the inner gate of the meadow and finding it without difficulty.

He was soon out of the meadow and in his own home where he found his mother asleep by a dying fire.

"Oh, Jan me son, the merry little Piskey men have paid 'ee out sure 'nough," said she when Jan had explained his long absence. " 'Tis a lesson to 'ee, my dear, and to all disbelievers like 'ee, not to doubt what you can't always see and understand. There are such strange things in this world of ours that I could never under-constumble why you would not believe in the Little People."

She shook her head as she looked at him. "Well, I never did hear of anybody ever before being kept fast in a Piskey ring, but I suppose they wanted to teach you a lesson."

"Which they have, mother, and one that I shall never forget as long as I live."

As Jan spoke, the sun began to silver the eastern sky over the moors. Glancing out of the window with a curious look in his gray eyes, Jan saw that the grass in Under-town meadow was a smooth green and the Piskey rings were no longer to be seen.

The Boy Who Played With the Piskeys

ON ONE OF THE St. Columb moors lived a woman who had a little boy. The boy was charming to look at, for his hair was as yellow as a day-old duckling and his eyes, which were large and dreamy, were the color of the speedwells that grew outside the thatched cottage that was his home.

But he was very lonely. He had no brothers or sisters and no one to play with. His mother had to work hard for her living and had small time to amuse her son even if she had realized how lonely he often was, which she did not.

"Go out on the moor and find playmates," she would say whenever he expressed his wish for playfellows.

One day, when Rafe was feeling lonelier than ever and his mother was too full of what she was doing even to talk to him, he said to himself, "I shall go out on the moor and see if I can find anybody to play with me." And he went.

It was in the springtime when the boy started off in search of playmates, and the great open spaces of the moor were full of color and sound. For the wasteland,

stretching miles and miles till it blended into blue distance, was a golden haze of gorse. Out of this burning
splendor came songs from moorland birds, and over it
rained music of caroling larks which sang far up in the
blue sky that domed the moor like a vast hyacinth.

The air was as full of fragrance as it was of song with
the peachlike smell of the furze bloom, while the more
pungent scent of the wild thyme was discernible when
the boy's hastening feet trod upon it and called it forth.
The pools here and there on the moor were as blue as
the sky they reflected, save where the overhanging willows and sweet gale made them dark and mysterious as
Piskeys' eyes.

The child wandered on, throwing his bright glances
about in search of someone or something to play with.

Once, when a lark rose from its nest in the turf and
went singing into the blue air, the little boy held up his
eager hands and called, "Skybird, come and play with
me!" But the skybird heeded him not.

Farther and farther from his mother's cottage Rafe
wandered, still casting wistful glances about him in the
hope of finding playmates.

Once, he heard a goldfinch singing its song from a
thornbush, so he stopped and listened. When the bird's
song was ended, it flew away toward a part of the moor

where streams abounded and the ground was marshy. The child followed it.

When Rafe had reached the marsh, he stood by its side and looked over it. It was full of marsh marigolds whose golden lamps lit the place; the marsh willows were in blossom; and on a low bank near where the boy stood was basking a little yellow lizard, or four-legged emmet, as the natives of the moor called it. The lizard looked almost as bright as the marsh flowers as it lay in the sun, and Rafe thought what a pretty thing it was. He took a step toward the bright creature, but it made haste to hide itself in the bushes.

Rafe stood by the marsh for ten minutes or more, looking at the marigolds and watching the clouds of pollen dust that fell from the willow catkins, wondering in his mind what made the little paths over the marsh so very green. These little paths were Piskey walks, although he did not know it, and Piskeys walked over them when the moon was high in the sky and even by day if they were so inclined.

As the boy stood gazing by the marsh, he heard the sound of tiny voices. The voices were so sweet and gay that he looked eagerly around to see whence the sound was coming. To his surprise and delight he saw a lot of Little People coming over the Piskey walks.

"Why, they are dinky men and women!" cried Rafe

to himself. "Not so big as the joanies I saw at St. Columb in Mister Bond's shop when mother took me there last market day." He looked more closely. "And they've got such handsome clothes on—just like gentry!"

The Little People seemed not to notice the child as they came tripping over the emerald-green paths, talking to each other. They were going toward a large, green circle a few yards up from the marsh where there was a low bank of feathery moss, ruddy green and gold. When they reached the bank, some of them sat down and others grouped themselves into a circle and began to play.

Rafe watched, all the time growing more and more excited. The game was fascinating to the little lonely boy who had wandered out on the moor in search of playmates, and so were the wonderful Little People who were playing it.

"They are so tiny and I am so big," he said to himself, "but I should like to play that game." Then, almost before he knew it, he had strolled up to the mossy bank where some of the Small People were sitting.

They watched the child advance, nor did they seem to resent his coming, but rather smiled as he came near.

"May I play with you?" Rafe asked, glancing from the Little People on the bank to those playing in the circle. "You are having such a beautiful game. I *should* love to play it with you."

108

"It is a Piskey game we are playing," said one of the dinky people in the circle, "and we ourselves are Piskeys."

"Are you?" said the boy. "I would so like to play your game with you. It must be nice to play with Piskeys." Then he added wistfully, "I have come down 'long here to find playmates 'cause I have none at home."

"We're very sorry for you," said one of the dinky men. "We're sorry for all children who have no playfellows."

"Then perhaps you will be my playmates!" cried Rafe joyously.

"We came over the walks on purpose to play with you," said a tiny man dressed in a scarlet cloak and hat. "We always know when boys and girls are lonely, and when it is possible we come and play with them, but it is not often possible."

"How is that?" asked the child.

"It is difficult to explain to a little boy like you. Grown-up people do not always think kindly of us and are sometimes even afraid of us. They say they do not like their children to play with us."

"How odd of them," said the child. "But my mother wouldn't mind, and she would let me play your pretty game. May I, please?"

"It is a long while since a child played with the Piskeys," piped a tiny man in a green coat and cap, "and

109

if you do you must not tell your mother that you played with us for the reason we have said."

"She won't ask me," said the child. "She is too busy to ask what I do out on the moor all day."

"Still, you must promise not to tell her," insisted the tiny man, "or we cannot let you play with us."

"Then I will promise," agreed the boy who was so eager to begin the game the Piskeys were playing.

"That is right," said the same little man, "but, remember, if you break your promise we will never play with you again. Now, come into the Piskey ring."

Scores of dinky hands, pretty as they were dinky, were stretched out to draw the willing child into the circle; and it was not long before the little lad's happy laugh was ringing out on the soft spring air, mingling with the gay laughter of the Small People.

After the boy and his new-found playmates had been playing for some time, the dinky man in the scarlet hat and green cloak told him that it was time to go back to his mother.

"I shall go if you will let me come and play with you again," said the child.

"You may come and play with us whenever you like as long as you do not break your promise," said the little man. "You will always find us in this spot."

110

BOY WHO PLAYED WITH PISKEYS

Rafe was reluctant to leave the Small People even to go home, but, seeing they wished him to, he went.

His mother had been very busy and did not ask what he had been doing with himself all day on the moor, and Rafe was glad that she did not.

Every day, whenever the weather was fine all through that spring and summer, the yellow-haired, blue-eyed boy went away over the great moor to play with the Piskeys; and every time he came home his mother never asked him where he had been nor how he had spent his time. Not that she was indifferent, but she believed he could not come to any harm on the moor.

Rafe was glad she did not ask him what he did with himself, not because he thought it was wrong to hide from her that he had been playing with the Piskeys, but because he dreaded to lose his little playfellows.

One day, after the child had again gone over the moor, his mother found she wanted wood to heat her cloam oven. Remembering that there was a great quantity of dried furze and brambles down by the marsh, she took a reaping hook and set out to cut some. As she left her cottage, she looked about for her boy to accompany her, but she could not see him anywhere.

The moor was flat save where it sloped up to the great rock-piled hills azure with mist. She could see over the open spaces for many miles, but not a glimpse of the child did she get, only a herd of horses streaking by in the wind.

"Where can Rafe have got to?" she asked herself as she looked this way and that. "I shall have to tell him he mustn't go out of my sight and hearing again. But I shan't stop here all day looking for him, or my oven won't be heated for want of wood."

The mother hastened over the moor, now glowing purple with heather. Still she glanced about in search of the child, but she never saw him. When she reached the place where the furze and brambles were very dry, she set to work to cut some. After she had cut all she wanted and was making it into a bundle, a ringing laugh broke upon her ear.

"That's my cheeld's laugh," she cried aloud. "The little scamp has never got down here, surely?"

Another gay little laugh came up from the right side of the marsh as she spoke. Dropping her furze bundle she hastened down to the marsh to see if she could see her child.

The character of the great marsh had wholly changed. It was different now from the time when the dreamy-eyed lad had stood on its edge gazing over it. The Piskey walks were still vividly green, but other flowers had succeeded the spring blossoms—bulrushes, velvety maces, and callow grass. There was not such a wealth of color

as when the marsh marigolds had glorified the place, but
the reeds and rushes and silvery cotton grass had a
beauty all their own, while the sudden flash of a dragon-
fly hovering over the sallows added a touch of brilliance.

It was very quiet. There was not a sound except a lark
singing in a cloud away over the moor. The silence after
the child's gay laugh made the woman nervous, and,
telling herself that she could not have heard aright, she
went back for her bundle of furze and then home.

Rafe returned to the cottage soon after his mother got
back. He was looking unusually happy. His face was in-
nocent and sweet, and he smiled to himself as an infant
does in its sleep.

"Where have you been off to?" asked his mother as he
came into the cottage.

"I've been out on the moor," he answered with the
same happy smile.

"I have been out on the moor too," she said, "but I did
not see you. I have been down near the marsh cutting
furze."

"Have you?" said the child, hardly noticing what she
said, for his thoughts were still with his playmates.

"Yes, and I wanted you to go with me. Where have
you been hiding yourself?"

"I did not hide myself anywhere," returned the boy.
"I was playing on the moor."

113

"What part of the moor?" his mother asked.

"Down near the big marsh," he answered.

"Then it *was* you I heard laughing!" she cried. "The marsh is not a safe place for a little chap like you to be all by yourself. There are long-cripples there and all sorts of things that might hurt you. You must not go there again."

"I don't go close to the marsh, not now," said the child, "and I am not afraid of long-cripples. They won't hurt me."

"All the same, you're not to go near the marsh," repeated his mother. "The moor is nice up here and full of flowers and berries."

"But it isn't so nice as down where I play. There are such lovely things down there where I go. I like being down there dearly."

"I should think you did by the way you were laughing. What were you laughing about? Was there anyone there with you?"

Rafe did not speak, but his little face went as scarlet as the dinky men's hats.

"Your face is a telltale," said his mother, eyeing him suspiciously. "You go down there to see somebody. Who is it, pray?"

Rafe said nothing.

"It's someone you are ashamed of and don't want your

114

own mother to know," she added as the boy still did not speak. "Who is it?"

"I must not tell," said the child.

"Not *tell?* Why not?"

"They said if I told they would never play with me again. We have such beautiful games together, mother, and I am never lonely now."

"*They!* Who're *they?*" asked his mother. "You will *have* to tell me," she commanded as the child looked troubled and would not answer. "You shall never go out on the moor again by yourself unless you tell me who it is you play with down by the marsh."

"It is the Little People who play with me," said the boy slowly, "dinky men and women."

"Little People! dinky men and women!" repeated the mother, aghast.

"They won't let me play with them any more," said the child mournfully. "They said they wouldn't if I told."

Rafe looked up at his mother, his blue eyes full of sorrow. Suddenly her own heart felt heavy as the bundle of furze she had brought in from the moor at the thought of what she had taken from her boy when she saw him looking so wisht.

"I'll play with you, little lad," she said softly, "and I'll not be so busy now neither."

Rafe never went to the marsh again for he knew he

would not find the Little People there, but he had not forgotten their game, and soon he taught it to his mother. And it was no uncommon sight for people passing near their cottage to see the two of them romping together, their laughter ringing out as gaily as the Piskeys' in the sweet moorland air.

The Spinning Plate

ON ONE OF THE wild carns of West Cornwall dwelt a clan of Piskey men. The moor between that carn and another almost as wild was a favorite place for their revels. On it they held their fairs and had their moonlight dances.

These Piskey men were a happy tribe, and one of their members was an especially merry person, as full of fun and mischief as he could hold together. His brother clansmen called him Little Man Antic. If there was any fun brewing, he was the brewer, if there were any pranks afoot, he was the ringleader. The Piskey men often told each other that their carn would be a very dull spot but for Little Man Antic.

One day in the early summer, the clan stood on top of the carn gazing out on the world. From that height they could command miles and miles of moorland; they could even see the sea in the distance, shining white in the eye of the sun. The Piskey men were very quiet until Little Man Antic broke the silence.

"I am inclined to have a joke with the man who lives in the cottage at the foot of our carn one of these odd days," he said. Then he turned to his brothers who were

117

gazing up at him, "Do you know the man I mean?"

"Of course we do," they answered. "We lived here in this carn before he was thought of."

"Why don't you have your joke now?" one of them pleaded.

"Yes, why not," said another, "for we have nothing at all to do today. Summer is a dull time of the year for folks like us. We can't lead people astray in broad daylight or play any proper tricks as it's hardly ever dark now, the sun rises so early and sets so late."

"No, I cannot have my bit of fun with the man now," said Little Man Antic shaking his head. "I must see how the land lies first."

"Tell us what your joke will be," cried the Piskey men eagerly.

"That would spoil the fun," answered Little Man Antic, "but it will be great fun, you'll see." Screwing up his dark, twinkling eyes till they were mere slits, he looked so absurdly funny that all the Piskey men roared with laughter.

"You are a joke yourself," cried a Piskey man, stroking his long, dark beard.

"I wish you were going to have your joke with the man now, this very minute," sighed another with a woebegone face. "I've nothing to do with myself."

"Then stand on your head," laughed Little Man Antic.

118

"If that doesn't please you, ride the billy goat that picks up his living on the carn, or wash your face in one of the rock basins here on the carn—it's quite dirty enough."

"I'll ride the billy goat willingly if you will have your joke on the man in the cottage today," the Piskey man answered.

"That I will," cried Little Man Antic. "We shall all ride him down toward the cottage. If the land lies properly I'll give you some fun today. Go and catch the animal at once. I'll ride on one of his horns, and the rest of you will ride bare-ridged."

The goat was caught, and soon the Piskey men were riding him down the rough side of the great, gray carn, winking and blinking, shouting and laughing as they rode; but only the goat heard the noise they made as he went like mad down the slope. When they neared the bottom, they jumped from the goat, who went scampering up the carn again.

"Now, you wait here while I see how things look," said Little Man Antic.

He was back in a minute or two, grinning and laughing and stroking his beard.

"Well?" said the Piskey men, looking eagerly at their brother. "Have you seen how the land lies?"

Little Man Antic nodded. "I have been down to the

119

cottage and peeped in. The miner is sound asleep in the kitchen, snoring away like old boots. His wife is in the front room knitting. It's a good time to have my bit of fun. Come along," he said, and the Piskey men nodded, smelling mischief as a mouse does cheese.

Skipping and hopping, Little Man Antic led the way, followed by the whole clan. They all hopped, skipped, and danced till they drew near the cottage, when they became suddenly quiet and walked softly.

The cottage was built of stone and thatched with yellow straw. Its casement windows and white door were flung wide to the moorland air. The back door opened into the kitchen, and on the drexel the Piskey men stood and looked in. The kitchen was large and in it were a granfer's clock, a table, two or three chairs, a high-backed settle, and an oaken dresser with its shelves full of china that shone in the sunlight.

In the elbowchair the miner was asleep, and there was no sound to be heard except his heavy breathing and the ticking of the clock.

"Is *that* the person you are going to have a joke with?" asked one of the Piskeys.

Little Man Antic nodded.

"But he is dead asleep and the last person in the world to have fun out of!"

120

"He won't be dead asleep long," chuckled a Piskey man, "if Little Man Antic is going to take him in hand."

"Will you tickle his nose or give him bad dreams or what?" asked a dozen Piskeys. "What are you going to do with him, Little Man Antic?"

"Nothing," Little Man Antic answered, winking and blinking and screwing up his eyes. Then he rounded his pliant body into a ball and rolled himself into the kitchen where the man was sleeping. When he had reached the middle of the room, he straightened himself up and beckoned to his brother Piskeys to come in.

Into the bright kitchen they all trooped, but their tiny brown feet made no sound on the hard granite floor as they came.

"You can sit or stand where you please," whispered Little Man Antic, "and the sooner you take your places the better."

"We'll take our places," said the clansmen, as some of them climbed up into the settle, sitting on its seat and arms, and some of them got up on the chairs and table, and the rest stood in little groups on the floor near the whitewashed walls.

Little Man Antic, his black eyes twinkling with merriment, did not go toward the miner as the Piskey men expected but made for the dresser. Having reached it he caught hold and swung himself up on the shelf, where he bowed solemnly to the Piskey men. They were, by now, getting more and more excited, not knowing what their brother was up to.

"Is it a new game?" they asked each other in whispers.

With another bow Little Man Antic turned his back on the wondering clan and calmly surveyed the long row of plates neatly arranged on the shelf. After gazing at them for a minute or more, he took one of them out. The plate made such a clatter, as it was meant to do, that it awoke the man in the chair. His face was a study as he saw the plate moving slowly across the dresser. Then he closed his eyes, shook his head hard from side to side, and opened them again, to see the plate approaching the edge of the dresser.

The Piskeys could hardly sit on the settle and chairs for excitement, while those standing on the floor were even more excited.

"What *is* our brother going to do with the plate?" one asked the other, their tiny dark eyes twinkling like stars on frosty nights.

Then, to their astonishment, they saw Little Man Antic climb down from the dresser with the plate.

"My ivers!" they cried, each Piskey man staring with all the eyes in his head. "Little Man Antic is bringing the great white plate down from the dresser, and the plate is almost as big as himself!"

"The best of the fun," said a much-whiskered Piskey, "is that the miner can see the plate coming down but he cannot see who is bringing it. Now he's wide awake like the day, watching his plate a-walking, and he cannot understand it."

"This is fun and no mistake," cried a hundred Piskey voices, but their voices were so soft that the sound of them might have been mistaken for the wind coming into the kitchen through the open windows and door.

"Do be quiet or you'll spoil the fun," said a Piskey man impatiently. "We can't talk and watch too. Be quiet or I'll pinch you."

"We'll be quiet for our own sakes," replied the Piskey men. "We'll be as still as the blades of grass when there is no wind to stir them."

They did as they said, and not one of them moved an eyelash as Little Man Antic slowly descended to the floor, gripping the great white plate. Laughing to themselves, each Piskey man kept one eye on the plate and the other on the miner, who was now sitting bolt upright in his chair, staring in open-mouthed astonishment.

The miner had not the gift of seeing the little invisible men, but his large white plate was very visible to him.

123

"My dear life!" he ejaculated at last, "my best cloam plate is clearly bewitched and is walking down from the dresser as if it had got a pair of legs."

The miner's exclamation sent the Piskey men into silent fits of laughter.

Little Man Antic reached the floor in safety, and when he had winked all round at his fellows and made a few grimaces, he trundled the plate till it came to the middle of the kitchen; then with another wink he began to whirl the plate till it went round and round like a spinning jenny.

"My plate is clean bewitched," cried the miner once more. Getting up from his chair he ran into the front room shouting, "Wife, wife, come here quick. Our best tea plate have a-come down from the dresser all by itself and is whizzing on the floor like mad!"

The Piskeys, hearing him, nearly burst their green coats with laughter, while one laughed so much that he tumbled off the arm of the settle on to his nose, dragging half a dozen others with him.

In the meantime Little Man Antic had stopped spinning the plate and had quickly rolled it over the floor and up the dresser, putting it back in its place. By the time the miner and his wife had reached the door, the kitchen was as quiet and peaceful as ever a Sunday morning could make it. The fresh moorland air came in the open windows, and the sunlight fell on the row of plates on the dresser.

"Did 'ee ever see anything like it in all your born days?" began the miner, when he saw there was nothing to be seen.

"Pack o' nonsense," said his wife. "Plates can't go a-spinning by themselves, that's certain, nor walk down from the dresser. You be dreaming surely."

She turned quickly and went back to her knitting in the front room. The miner scratched his head and sat down in his chair, but no sooner had he done so than Little Man Antic trundled the plate down from the dresser and began spinning it again on the floor.

The miner watched in amazement. "A spirit of mischief have got into the plate," he muttered to himself. "I've heard tell of such things when the Piskeys come down from the carn and enter folks' houses to play them tricks. Now wife must believe me this time," and again he went running out of the kitchen, calling to her to come quickly.

When she came the kitchen was still as before, and everything was in its place. Perhaps the wind was making more of a rustling sound, but if it was she was far too cross to hear it.

"Pack o' nonsense," she said, "disturbing me at my

125

work with your talk of Piskeys. Piskeys indeed! Why, little bits of chaps like they couldn't spin a plate. What's more, if there were any in our cottage we should see or hear them."

She turned to the miner, who was standing in the doorway rubbing his eyes. Suddenly she picked up a broom from the hearth and held it up to him. "Be off with you now and let the moorland air wash the nonsense from your eyes."

The miner ran from the cottage, and his wife ran after him, shaking the broom before her.

"Quick," Little Man Antic cried.

Every Piskey ran for a plate, and when the miner's wife came back to her kitchen, hot and breathless and very cross, she saw every plate on the dresser spinning round and round on the floor. Her eyes got bigger and bigger until they were almost as big as the plates. When the plates stopped whirling and by themselves rolled back to the dresser and climbed up its red-painted sides to their places on the shelves, she could stand it no longer. Throwing her apron over her head, she ran out onto the moor, calling to her husband to save her from the Piskeys.

"Well, did I succeed?" asked Little Man Antic as he and his brothers ascended the slopes of the carn.

126

THE SPINNING PLATE

"That you did," cried the Piskey men. "It was the best bit of fun we've had for many a day. It was enough to make a goat laugh, it was!"

Little Man Antic made no reply. He was busy thinking up the next joke he would play.

Bucca Boo's
Little Merry Men

NEARLY EVERYBODY IN Mevagissey had heard of
Bucca Boo, the Neptune of the Cornish sea, and how he
had commanded his nine little mermen to row in their
longboat to a large rock pool near one of Mevagissey's
high cliffs. There, cormorants and gulls nested, and a
rare weed called the Weed of Health grew. The Mevagissey people had also heard that whoever was lucky
enough to see the wonderful little boat, curved like a
moon on her back, and bring her inside Mevagissey
Quay would bring good luck to himself and the whole
fishing town.

No one believed the old whiddle any more except
Merlin Legassick, an ancient fisherman, and his grandson and namesake. Old Merlin declared that his great-
granfer had seen such a boat come into the basin, but
as he was crippled in his legs he could not climb up the
slippery sides of the rock and so lost the chance of getting the little craft and bringing her into the quay.

This old whiddle had made a great impression on the
younger Merlin, and it was the one desire of his heart to
see the little boat his great-great-grandfather had seen,
so he watched for her coming at each flow of the tide.

129

PIXIE FOLKLORE

In those days the people of Mevagissey were all fisher-folk and exceedingly poor owing to the scarcity of fish. Most of them knew, more often than not, the pangs of hunger. Old Merlin Legassick and his children and grandchildren were some of the worst sufferers, as they were a large family and, being so many to share the little food there was, they had often to go supperless to bed.

As the fishing grew worse and worse, Merlin the elder and Merlin the younger longed more and more for the coming of the little boat into Bucca Boo's Basin, for it would turn the luck of the fishing from bad to good if only one of them could see her there and get hold of her. But, in spite of all their watching and longing, she had not yet come into the pool.

The younger Merlin was beginning to despair of her ever coming at all. The elder Merlin was often a bit down in the mouth too, only he would not allow it and cheered his little grandson by telling him that she was bound to put into the basin sometime, adding impressively, " 'Tis a prize worth waiting for even if she don't come till you be as ould and grayheaded as your granfer."

Neither Merlin went fishing. The old man was too feeble and the boy too young, but the former mended the fishing nets, and the little lad got the bait to supply the hooks. Late one afternoon in the beginning of June when

the larks were thrilling the blue air with their melodies
and Mevagissey cliffs were a sight to see, with the pink
of the thrifts and the red and gold of the lady's fingers,
old Merlin sent his namesake to Polstreath beach to dig
sprats in the great stretch of sand there.

As the lad was leaving the cottage on the cliffside, the
ancient grandsire begged him to keep an extra lookout
for the dinky longboat.

" 'Tis such handsome weather," he said, "an' the sea
from Rame's Head to Chapel Point is like a millpond
a'most. Whichever way the little merry men be pleased
to come, they will be able to get into the bay as easy as
any of our own boats."

Old Merlin's manner was so eager and his voice so
earnest that the boy, instead of going to Polstreath as
he was bidden, went to Bucca Boo's Basin. When he
got there the tide had not yet reached the rock where
the pool was, but it was flowing fast toward it. The sea
was rougher than his grandfather had allowed him to
expect, and waves were breaking against the northern
cliffs, which were by far the boldest in the bay.

"The wee chaps and their dinky longboat won't come
today, that's certain," said the boy to himself, a look of
disappointment on his bright young face as he stood
gazing seaward. "If they don't make haste granfer an'

131

me won't be alive to watch, for we shall soon die of hunger, an' all the other folk in Mevagissey will, too."

The words were hardly out of his mouth when a laugh from somewhere close to him stole upon his ear. At first he thought it was the giggle of a kittiwake, which often laughs as it flies over the cliffs, but as it was followed by a chorus of tiny voices singing he knew it could not be. Much wondering what it was, young Merlin listened intently, and as he listened it dawned upon him that it *might* be Bucca Boo's little merry men come into the basin at last.

No sooner had this idea taken possession of his mind than he climbed up the side of the rock and peeped into the pool. There, to his unspeakable delight, was a tiny boat not much bigger than a child's toy and curved like a moon on her back. The little craft was full of tiny men with scarlet caps on their dark heads, for all the world like inverted sea anemones. Jumpers clung tight to their slim figures which, when they moved, were all sparkle and color like a mackerel's back.

" 'Tis the boat I've been on the lookout for all this time," young Merlin said joyfully to himself as he watched her riding on the emerald-green water under the shadow of the basin's side, "an' my chance is come at last to bring good luck to Mevagissey and the fishing!"

As he said this, wondering how he could get hold of

132

the tiny craft, all the little men began laughing and chaffing each other. Then one of them broke out into a rollicking song with a chorus in which they all joined.

> "With a dally rally O!
> With a rally dally O!
> In their longboat O!"

Merlin, as he listened, could scarcely refrain from joining in, too, the air was so catching and as fresh as the breeze blowing in from the sea.

When they had finished their song, they gripped their oars and began to row the boat across the pool to where Merlin was looking over it, motionless as the basin itself. Merlin held his breath as she came, waiting to grip her when she got under the basin's brim. The dinky crew were so intent on their rowing that they did not notice the brown handsome face of the lad who was watching them. When the boat was within a yard or so from where Merlin was sitting, the little man at the helm suddenly pointed to something glowing like flame under the rim of the basin.

"It is the Weed of Health," he cried.

"So it is," responded all the little men, suspending their golden oars to gaze at the burning weed.

"How are we to get it?" asked one anxiously.

"That's the question," replied the helmsman. "If I can

measure distance with my eye, I'm afraid it is far out of our reach."

"In that case our coming here is all in vain," said one of the crew in a dismal voice. "Our Bucca Boo will never be himself again, and that horrid Bee Bo will sit on the great pearl throne instead."

"It is terrible to think of," said another. "If only we had legs made for climbing, as those great men-creatures have who live in yonder town," he sighed, turning his face in the direction of Mevagissey.

"Do not look at the black side of things until you are so obliged," the helmsman commented severely.

"Let's go and have a closer view," piped a little voice. "It may not be so un-get-at-able as we fear."

"Yes, let us," they all cried.

When Merlin saw the boat turn round and make for the spot where the weed was burning as bright as a field of poppies, he pulled himself back very gently and crept round to where the little craft was close in to the basin's wall. As soon as he dared peep over the pool, he saw that the little merry men were looking anything but merry. Gazing at each other in silent dismay, they sat for five minutes or more, when a voice broke the silence with a cry of hope.

"Why, how stupid we are! The sea will flow into the basin soon after sundown, and the basin will be so full

134

of water that it will be easy to reach the beautiful weed."

"You forget that the weed blossoms and ripens only two hours before the sun posts westward," said the steersman sadly, "and it is within half an hour of that time now."

"I had forgotten that," the small man murmured.

"And we must therefore give up all hope of taking back the Weed of Health to our dear Bucca Boo," piped another little voice, wisht as the cry of a gull proclaiming a storm.

"We shall never dare show our faces in Bucca Boo Town without the weed," said an oarsman, shaking his scarlet-capped head. "I, for one, could not bear to see the despair in Bucca's eyes nor the look of triumph in Bee Bo's. Bee must have known when we sailed away to this place that the Weed of Health was growing where we feetless little men could never get it."

When Merlin, who was a feeling-hearted little chap, heard what Bucca Boo's nine merry men said, he felt sorry for them and almost lost sight of his own troubles in theirs. The moment, however, they stopped talking and sat looking at each other, the thought of the hungry ones in Mevagissey came over him. Telling himself that now was his opportunity to bring good luck to everybody in the little fishing town, he crooked his bare feet in the

135

PIXIE FOLKLORE

outer rim of the basin and let himself gently down its
seaweed-covered side.

As he hung head downward his full length and was
stretching out his hands to grasp the boat, one of her
crew looked up and saw him. He uttered a cry of warning, and in a moment of time the boat and her crew were
far from the boy's outflung hands. Merlin pulled himself
up from his undignified position amid roars of laughter
from the nine little merry men.

"You thought you had got us nicely, didn't you?" asked
the helmsman, doffing his bright cap in derision. "Perhaps you will be a bit slower in your movements the
next time Bucca Boo's merry men in their longboat come
into the basin."

"I can get you now if I like," cried Merlin, who was
a quick-tempered lad and did not at all like the way the
little cock-a-hoop spoke to him. "I can dive like a shag
and swim like a fish, and if I dive down there into the
pool I can get you quite easily. It was only the fear of
upsetting your little craft an' drowning 'ee all that
stopped me. There now!"

The nine little merry men seemed vastly amused at
the boy's boast and laughed till the salt tears rolled down
their faces.

"It is quite too funny," cried one, wiping his eyes on
the hem of his jumper.

136

"Yes, isn't it?" cried another. "Fancy his being afraid of *our* drowning!" and again they roared with laughter.

" 'Tis no laughing matter," shouted Merlin, who was red as a boiled crab with anger. "I'll spring into the pool now and get 'ee."

"Do!" taunted the helmsman, who was evidently the spokesman of the longboat crew and a person of some importance. "But I think you will have as much difficulty in laying hold of our boat as you would of its reflection."

"I'll come all the same," cried the boy, diving into the pool as he spoke.

When Merlin came to the top of the water, the little craft was nowhere to be seen. After swimming about in the basin looking for the lost boat under all the seaweed and into every hole where he thought it was possible for so tiny a craft to hide, he reluctantly came to the conclusion that Bucca Boo's little merry men and their longboat had vanished forever.

It was a crestfallen lad that climbed up the basin's side, low spirited indeed to think that he had had the chance of bringing good luck to his town and had lost it by his hasty temper and boasting. Like the merry men, he felt he could not go home and face his family and friends after missing such a splendid opportunity.

As he sat on the basin's brim with his bare legs dangling over, feeling as miserable as a gull with its wings clipped, a gurgle broke on his ear—just the sort of gurgle that had made him think of the laugh of the kittiwake half an hour before. It came *up* from the pool and, looking down, Merlin saw to his amazed delight the tiny longboat and its crew in their scarlet caps and shining jumpers. They were in the very spot where they had so strangely disappeared.

"So you are not so clever as you thought you were!" chorused the little merry men in voices which sounded like a company of hedge sparrows chirping.

"No," said the boy honestly, "I en't. And what is worse still, I'm afraid now I shall never get hold of 'ee an' bring good luck to our fishing."

"Whatever do you mean?"

So Merlin told them all about the strange whiddle, finishing up by saying that he supposed it wasn't a bit true and that the poor folks of Mevagissey would still go to bed with empty stomachs.

"Part of the story is true enough, or we would not be here in the basin now," said the helmsman, looking up not unkindly at the boy's sad face. "The rest of the story was born of a despairing hope in a man-creature's brain pan. I am sorry for you nevertheless," he added after a pause, "but you see it is quite useless to hope that you or anybody could ever bring us and our boat inside Mevagissey Quay *against* our will."

138

He took his gaze from the disconsolate lad as he was speaking and again looked with longing eyes at the weed almost touching the boy's bare legs. Merlin followed the glance, and, noticing the hopelessness of its expression, a kind thought came into his mind.

Leaning over the pool he said, "As it don't seem in my power to bring prosperity to our poor little Mevagissey an' make the folks there happy, I'll make you an' your Bucca Boo happy instead, if I can."

"You! What can you do to make us and our dear Boo happy?" asked all the nine little men in great amazement.

"I heard you talking just now 'bout the Weed of Health," answered the boy, touching the glowing fronds which, since he had climbed up on the basin's brim a second time, had put forth silvery looking berries with streakings of crimson and gold. "I heard you say you was in a terrible way 'cause it grew where you couldn't reach it."

The little men were listening with all their ears, watching the boy intently.

"Well," Merlin went on, "it has just come into my noddle that I can pick it for you, that is, if you will please let me, little misters."

"Will you really do that kindness for us and our Boo?"

139

they asked eagerly, hope and delight spreading over their faces.

"Iss, of course I will," answered the boy. "Tell me when you want it picked, and I'll do it for 'ee."

The nine little men talked to each other, speaking so low that Merlin couldn't catch a word they said; besides, he was too much Nature's gentleman and a Cornishman to bend over and listen. They were holding a kind of privy council and were apparently of one mind, for when they had finished their say the little oarsmen straightened themselves, and the steersman stood up in the stern of the boat and saluted the boy after the manner of royal boatmen.

"In the name of his majesty, Bucca Boo of the Cornish Sea, we gratefully accept your kind offer to gather him the Weed of Health which we have come so far to get. At the same time we make you an offer under certain conditions, and, if you will fulfill them, we will allow you to take us in our longboat inside Mevagissey Quay and so bring good luck to the fishing there."

"Do 'ee really an' truly mean what you say?" gasped Merlin, almost tumbling into the pool in his excitement.

"Yes, really and truly," responded the steersman with a broad grin. "But under certain conditions," he nodded again impressively.

"What be they, little misters?" asked the boy.

140

BUCCA BOO'S LITTLE MERRY MEN

"The conditions are that the moment you have gathered the Weed of Health and its berries and dropped it into the pool you will leave here at once. Return to your town or its neighborhood and there remain until we have rowed up to your quay, which we will do just before the tide turns. Come down to the quay then and bring the boat inside."

Merlin was about to speak, but the steersman went on. "In the meantime," he said, "you must not tell anybody, not even your parents, of our being here in the basin or that you have the power to bring good cheer to everybody in your town."

"Is that all you want me to promise?" asked the boy. "I reckon I can do that." Then he added with a broad smile, "It will be as easy as walking."

"Not so easy as you think," said the helmsman gravely. "You will be tempted to tell everyone you meet that you have seen Bucca Boo's nine little merry men in their longboat and that they have promised you to come up to the quay at the turning of the tide. Remember, if you do tell anyone your chance of bringing good luck to your town will be gone forever."

Merlin nodded solemnly, "I'll remember."

"Another thing we shall warn you against," the little man went on. "Should you be tempted, as you probably will, to detain our boat when you have brought us into your quay, you will be in danger of changing the good luck to bad. If you keep us against our will, even for an hour, Bucca Boo will turn all your fishing nets into boulders and your lines into stones."

"I won't tell the folks for anything if you don't want me to," said Merlin. "But I should like to tell my old granfer, who do take much interest in 'ee all. It will be dreadful hard not to tell him."

"Nevertheless you may not tell even your granfer until you have taken us into the quay. You may then. But now," the steersman spoke more briskly, "if you are willing to gather the weed, please be quick. It is ripe and ought to be plucked at once both for your sake and for our own. The waves are beginning to dash against the foot of the rock."

"I forgot the tide," cried Merlin, flinging himself flat on the basin's brim and gathering the scarlet weed with its bright berries. He plucked all there was and dropped it into the pool, then, as the little merry men were stowing it away in their longboat, he climbed down the basin's side.

If he had been five minutes later, he would not have been able to get away from the great rock at all for it was almost surrounded by the sea. Once clear of the rock Merlin made for Mevagissey. Distantly he heard the little merry men singing at the top of their voices the song which had so delighted him. Running up the narrow streets of the little town, Merlin found himself singing too and with as much gusto as the merry men.

Everyone he met asked what was the matter with him and Merlin had, as the steersman foretold, the greatest difficulty in the world to keep from telling that he had seen with his own eyes Bucca Boo's little merry men in their longboat and of all the luck and cheer the town was going to have. When he reached home his grandfather quickly saw that something out of the ordinary had happened to the boy and plied him with questions.

Merlin would have answered the old man's questions gladly, but he dared not because of what the helmsman had said to him. To prevent himself from letting out all there was to tell, he contorted his face so that his grandsire thought he was either making faces at him on purpose or that he really had seen the longboat in the rock pool and let go his chance of bringing her up to the quay. Old Merlin threatened the boy that if he did not let him hear all there was to hear he would give him the rope's end.

"You have bewitched the cheeld with your nonsense about Bucca Boo's little boat coming into our bay," struck in the lad's mother after looking at her son. "Shame to 'ee, Granfer Legassick."

When the angry old man insisted that it was his belief

143

the boy had seen the longboat and wouldn't tell, young Merlin to escape further questioning took to his heels and made for the top of the hill above the town where he knew his grandfather could not follow him.

The sun was sinking behind Mevagissey by this time, and all the beauty of the evening sky was reflected in the quiet waters of the bay. The whole harbor was lovely with reflected light, and even the northern cliffs shone with gold. As the sun sank lower and lower, the fishing boats came up the bay, catching the light on their weather-stained sails.

The lad watched the boats moving toward the quay, and as they came he saw the women and children go down on the quay walls to welcome them back and to see if they had a good catch of fish. But Merlin could tell by the very movements of the people that the fishermen's luck had been bad again.

"I'm glad as a bird that I didn't let out to anybody, nor to granfer nuther, that I saw the dinky longboat in Bucca Boo's Basin," said the lad to himself as his brown eyes followed the people on their homeward way, "for now there won't be any more starving folks in Mevagissey Town after tonight when I shall have brought the little craft and all her merry men into our quay!" He clapped his hands for the joy of it, then clapped them over his mouth lest he should be heard.

144

"Aw, I wonder what granfer an' all of 'em will say to me," he went on softly to himself, "when they have heard what I have seen with my own two eyes an' done with my own two hands. And that I, Merlin Legassick, have brought good luck to the fishing and good cheer to the people in our town." He laughed aloud at the thought of it.

The sun had dropped behind the hill by this time, but the clouds that stretched across the sky from Mevagissey to Goran Churchtown still held the sunlight. When the sun had set and the afterglow had all gone and the little town, lying low in the valley below where Merlin sat, grew indistinct in the semi-darkness, the lad got up and went down the hill.

Mevagissey people went early to bed, and the narrow, twisting streets were very quiet as the lad made his way through them. His own people had retired even before the sun went down. Poor dears, they had nothing cheering to make them want to sit up. The catch of fish was unusually bad, not more than one small fish to a boat, and they all felt very miserable. Saying bed was the best place for starving people, to bed the Legassicks had gone, leaving the door on the latch for little Merlin.

When the lad reached home he found even his old grandfather abed and apparently fast asleep, much to his

145

thankfulness, for there was no one to ask him troublesome questions.

It was yet a good while to the ebb of the tide, but Merlin was loath to go to sleep, fearing he should not wake in time. He shared his room with several of his brothers, and, as he lay listening to their heavy breathing, a terrible misgiving took possession of him that Bucca Boo's little merry men had tricked him. The idea made him so miserable that he got into his clothes and crept out into the little street.

He had no sooner left the house than a pair of old eyes looked out of the window, watching eagerly to see what way the boy would go.

Once out on the street Merlin raced down to the quay and arrived there breathless. It was later than he thought, for a clock in the distance was striking the hour, and Merlin knew that the tide had already turned. There was still a great deal of ground swell on outside the little haven, but inside, where all the fishing boats were riding in safety, it was like a lake. The boy peered anxiously over the quay, but he could see nothing save the water heaving against its stone walls.

"I don't believe they meant to come when they sent me off like that," the boy cried aloud. " 'Twas a dirty trick to play on a poor little chap like me. I would a-kept my word."

146

BUCCA BOO'S LITTLE MERRY MEN

"And we have kept ours," cried a little voice sweet and clear as a blackbird's whistle.

It was followed by a burst of hearty laughter, and, looking down again, Merlin saw on the dark water the longboat and her crew shining like a rising star.

"Aw, I *am* so glad you've come," exclaimed the boy, leaning over the quay wall in a transport of delight. "I was afraid you had gone along home. Shall I come down now an' bring the little boat an' you into the quay?"

"Have you kept your promise?" asked the steersman.

"Iss, faithful," answered the boy.

"Then come down at once and bring Bucca Boo's merry men inside Mevagissey Quay and win for the fisherfolk prosperity forever."

Young Merlin was down the quay's stone stairway in a jiffy. When he was about to lay his hands on the tiny boat and her crew, he paused, partly from fear and partly because she looked so beautiful: one moment she was a curve of crimson flame seeming to catch the water on fire around her and the next she was like a rainbow lying on its back.

"Don't be afraid to touch the longboat," cried the nine little merry men. "She'll hurt nobody who plucked the scarlet Weed of Health. Be quick, please, for there is a faraway sound of an old man walking along the street."

For the sake of his beloved town and its people, Mer-

147

lin took hold of the glowing little boat and brought her safely inside Mevagissey Quay. There she lay, a burning wonder on the quiet water, by the side of his father's fishing boat.

"Now," said the helmsman, standing up in the stern of the dinky craft, "speed away to meet the old man and tell him that at last Bucca Boo's little merry men have been brought inside Mevagissey Quay, and that the hand which brought her and us has won good luck to Mevagissey fishing forever."

"Don't send me away please, dear little sirs," pleaded the boy. "Let me keep the longboat here in the quay till the morning that the folks may see with their own eyes what a beauty she is with her dinky golden oars and all."

"Away," said the little man sternly, "unless you wish to undo the blessing you have brought for this place and bring it a curse instead. Remember what we told you."

It was hard for Merlin to leave the little craft, which seemed to grow more and more beautiful as he gazed at it. Then he remembered all that he and the poor people in his town had suffered, and he made himself withdraw his gaze. Having done that, his passionate desire to detain her left him, and he rushed away to tell his grandfather, whom he saw walking toward him as quickly as his aged feet would let him.

BUCCA BOO'S LITTLE MERRY MEN

"I guessed what was in the wind," said old Merlin, thumping his grandson's back in his joy when he had told him the great news. "An' you was a sensible little chap to keep it dark, especially as they little merry men didn't want us to know."

He took young Merlin's hand in his. "Come along to the quay head," he said eagerly. "Maybe having give 'ee permission to tell me, they will wait by the quay that I may have the chance of seeing her."

The hope was vain. When they got to the quay and looked in, there was nothing to be seen except the fishing fleet riding on the dark, still water in their safe anchorage.

"An' she was down here by father's boat only ten minutes or so ago, burning like the moon away there," cried young Merlin, gazing out toward the sea, "an' now she is nowhere to be seen. 'Tis queer, sure 'nough."

"There is something or other glowing like a live coal on the horizon," said the old man, also gazing seaward where the moon was rippling the water. "Is it a star low down on the sea or is it the dinky longboat an' the nine little merry men going back home?"

It was a question young Merlin could not answer, and neither he nor the old fisherman was ever sure what the nature of that soft glow on the water's edge was. As they turned away from the quay, the wind blowing in from the open sea brought with it the sound of voices singing way faraway. The boy, listening with all his ears, thought he heard the last lines of the little merry men's song—

> "With a dally rally O!
> With a rally dally O!
> In their longboat O!"

All Mevagissey was in a ferment of excitement the next morning when young Merlin's story was noised about. Some believed it and some did not. Others declared that he had dreamed it all.

"True or not true, time will tell," said the old Merlin laconically. "But if it be true that Bucca Boo's nine little merry men and their dinky longboat have been in the rock pool and that my dear grandson and namesake saw her with his own eyes and brought her inside our quay, then prosperity has come to us."

If they laughed at the old man, as they had so often, he would nod and say, "You will all be wishing soon 'twas your eyes saw the little craft and your hands that brought her hither."

Young Merlin's story was soon verified, for, from the night that the lad declared the longboat and her crew had ridden safely on the water of Mevagissey Harbor, prosperity came to the little fishing town, to its fisher-

BUCCA BOO'S LITTLE MERRY MEN

folk, and particularly to the House of Legassick which flourished amazingly. If fish stayed away from the nets and lines of other Cornish fishermen, they did not from the fishermen of Mevagissey, and there was never any more need for anybody to go to bed with an empty stomach,

The Gnome Maiden

LONG AGO THERE lived in the interior of the Morwenstow hills a gnome and his wife. They had a little daughter who was white of skin and very beautiful and whose name was Tamara.

There were giants in the land in those days, and the gnomes hated the giants. They did not want the giants ever to see their lovely Tamara, for they were afraid that if they saw her they would steal her heart from them. So the gnomes told themselves that Tamara should never see the light of day if they could prevent it.

When the gnome child was old enough to ask the reason of this and that, she wandered one day into an outer cave which had a crack in the roof. As she happened upon it, a ray of silvery light shone through the crack, and Tamara thought she had never seen anything so wonderful before. She ran back to her mother to ask her what it was.

"It is only a beam of brightness," answered the gnome mother, troubled that her child should have gone into the outer cave while the sun was glinting into it.

"What is brightness?" asked the gnome child.

153

"Brightness is a child of the great white fire that warms the world above our own."

"I did not know there was another world," said Tamara. "I want to go up and see it and play with Little Brightness."

"That is impossible," said her mother. "Gnomes who live under the hills have nothing in common with the upper world."

"Tamara is tired of playing with Tamara," the gnome child said wistfully. "Could you not ask Little Brightness to come and play with me?"

"That I cannot do," the gnome mother replied. "If Tamara wants playmates, she has them in Little Shadows. They are always ready for a game when the fire burns on the floor of our cavern."

"I do not like Little Shadows," cried Tamara, "and I will not play with them any more!"

But she did, all the same, for when Tamara was tired of playing with herself she turned to the shadows who dwelt in the crannies of the walls and came out to dance on them when the gnomes lit their fire. Tamara played and danced and was happy and gay as any gnome child.

Time went on, and her mother hoped she had forgotten Little Brightness. But she had not, and whenever her parents were busy and unobservant Tamara went into the outer cavern to look for the child of the great white sun. If she saw Little Brightness peeping through the roof crack, she was glad and sang her a gnome song which her mother had taught her; but if Little Brightness was not there, Tamara's heart was sad. More often than not she was not there, for the sunbeam only glinted into the darkness of the cave at certain times of the year.

When Tamara had grown to be a tall maiden and had not seen the bright beam of light for a long time, she asked her mother if Little Brightness was too old to peep through cave cracks as she herself was now too old to play with Little Shadows.

"Perhaps so," returned the gnome mother.

The gnome father said it was more than likely that the child of the great white fire was already wed to one of her kind and had now something better to do than to peek through cavern holes. "It is time to seek a son of the gnomes to wed with our Tamara," he added.

The gnome maiden would not hear of such a thing and declared that if she ever wedded it would be to one as fair as Little Brightness.

"It is time you forgot the white fire's child and thought of more important matters," said her father.

"I will never forget Little Brightness," cried Tamara, "nor shall I rest till I have seen her and the upper world where she dwells."

"The world of which you speak so glibly is not easy

to find," said the gnome father gravely, "and it is full of evil things. Giants dwell in it, and some of them live on the tors not far from the hill in whose heart is our home. If these giants were to behold you, they might take you from us."

"You tell me that the upper world is not easy to find," replied the gnome maiden, in no way frightened at what her parent had said, "but since it can be found there must be a way up to it. Tell me the way, please, my father?"

"I will not tell you," he said sternly. "We have kept you in ignorance of the way all your life for we know what the world above is like and that in every corner of it evil lurks. Be content to dwell in this safe under-world with your mother and me, who love you better than you know."

The beautiful daughter of the gnomes was not content and took no heed of her parents' warning. Having learned that there was a way up to the world above, she told herself that she would find it. So, one day, when her mother and father were occupied with their own affairs, Tamara went on stealthy feet out of her cavern home, unnoticed save by Little Shadows.

"I shall not return to the cave where I came into being until I have found the way to the upper world," said the gnome maiden to herself as she wandered from cave to cave and from passage to passage in the dark underworld.

After much seeking she chanced upon a passage that twisted and turned and turned and twisted but all the time led upward. Tamara followed it and after a long climb found herself in a large cavern into which light was shining.

"It is the mouth of the upper world," she cried and ran forward till she came to the outer opening which looked across a moor.

The cavern faced the sunrise. Across the far-reaching moor Tamara saw a great flame burning against a sky of many colors. It was the dawn on which she gazed, and the red sun was rising between the tors which loomed dark and large on either side. This was all she saw, for the moor was only emerging from the darkness of the night. But she had seen enough, for the vision of the daybreak and the rising sun filled her gnome mind with amazement kin to terror, and she fled back to the underworld.

The gnomes had missed their child and guessing where she had gone were on the point of seeking her when she came rushing into the cavern.

"Where have you been—running so fast and with a face so fearful?" asked the gnome father.

157

Tamara, still frightened and trembling, answered, "To the mouth of the other world and back again."

"It was wrong of you to go anywhere without our knowledge and consent," her father said, "especially to places where dangers lurk and evil is abroad."

"What did you see from the mouth of the cave?" the gnome mother asked.

Tamara answered slowly, "A great place with walls very beautiful and high, bright like the smiles of Little Brightness. Up against the walls were rocks, dark like the walls of our cavern. Between them burned a red fire which did not spurt like our little one but rose steadily up. That was all I saw, but it made me afraid, so I returned to you and to this dark place."

"It is a safe place even though it is dark," her mother said reprovingly, "and it is not full of dangers as is that strange world above us."

"It is well for you that it was only daybreak when you looked out from the upper cave," muttered the gnome father. "If it had been later in the day the giants of whom we have warned you and still warn you would have been abroad and might have seen you. Go no more, my child, to the world so fair and yet so full of evil to one as beautiful as you are."

Tamara said nothing, for even in the midst of her fears she longed to look again upon the world of light. She

158

watched her opportunity to slip away, and one day when her parents were busy she stole out of the cavern and made her way up the long dark passage.

The sun had been up some time and was marching across the heavens. It was springtime, and the great moor was a symphony of color and sound. The broom was in flower and so was the gorse, and from bush and brake came gushes of song. Linnets and thrushes piped and fluted, as did the yellowhammers, golden feathered like the bushes from which they sang, while out of the warm air came showers of melody from larks atremble with their own music.

There were other sounds too, the buzz of bees and the soft voice of the wind blowing over the turf and the flowers. The moor spread away to the east where the tors were as blue as the veronicas already in blossom under the shelter of granite boulders. Westward where the sun was marching was a flock of clouds, white and glistening and soft as thistledown. They were shepherded by the wind which drove them eastward toward the tors.

The gnome maiden saw it all, and her young body trembled like a leaf. The vision of the vast moor fascinated her, and the melody of innumerable birds filled her with delight. Yet, still she was afraid.

For a long time she gazed and listened, but it never

159

entered her gnome mind to step out on the moor until her dark eyes saw shadows flying over the heather in front of the wind-driven clouds. The shadows, she thought, must be near of kin to Little Shadows down in her cavern home. They were the only familiar things on the moor, and the sight of them took away her fears. Out of the cavern she stepped, and in another minute she was racing after the shadows, shouting to them to stop.

The dark flying shadows did not stop. On and on they went toward the tor country, and on and on the gnome maiden flew after them. Over the springing heather and sweet smelling thyme she went, and never once did she stop until her swift feet were suddenly arrested by the sight of two young men coming down the slopes of the hill toward her.

"They are the giants of whom my father told me," she cried aloud to herself, too frightened to move. When they came near enough to see her, she turned and fled.

"Have you been again to the mouth of the upper world?" her father asked angrily as Tamara entered the cavern.

"I have," she answered.

"And what did you see this time?"

Answering slowly the gnome maiden said, "Wonderful things. I saw the great white fire moving under the blue roof of the upper world."

160

"What else did you see?" demanded the gnome father still more angrily.

"Many things very strange and beautiful, and I heard sweet sounds that thrilled me."

"What sounds?" asked the gnome mother.

"I cannot tell," Tamara replied, "but they came up from the floor of the great cavern and down from its roof."

"Was that all you heard and saw?" asked the gnome mother, her eyes troubled.

"No," returned Tamara. "I saw some near relations of Little Shadows, and I ran out of the mouth of the world to have a game with them."

"What then?" asked her father gloomily.

"As I ran over the yielding floor of the world, I saw two creatures coming with mighty strides toward me," replied the gnome maiden with something new in her voice that made her parents look at each other. "They were very tall and straight and had hair the color of the bright bushes from which sweet sounds were pouring. They looked at me as you, my parents, do when you are pleased with your Tamara."

"What next?" asked the gnome father with a dreadful look on his face.

"I turned my back on them and ran till I reached the mouth of the upper world—"

"It is well," the gnome father said hastily, "that there is a cavern in the underworld for you to flee, to where giants may not come. The sight of those men-creatures, the sons of the giants, will, no doubt, prevent you from going to the upper world again."

"Perhaps so," said Tamara, but the look in her eyes and the soft sound in her voice told her mother that she would escape to the world above at the first opportunity.

"A strange maiden is our Tamara," said the gnome father when Tamara went to talk with Little Shadows. "She is as unlike us as light is from darkness. I cannot understand her. She revels in the light as we do in the gloom."

"That is true," answered the mother sadly. "Our beautiful daughter possesses something we do not possess. She is like the pond lily's babe who, when it is conscious of life within its brown bulb as it lies in the bottom of the pool, yearns to unfold its beauty in the light and is ever pushing upward till it reaches the surface of the water to lie cradled in the sun."

"True," said the gnome father, "but the lily's child, when the sun has set, slides down to the bottom of the pool; our child, when she has seen a little more of the upper world, will never return to us again."

The handsome young giants and the wonders of the upper world were constantly in Tamara's thoughts, so

162

one day when the gnomes were unwatchful she went softly out of the cavern. With quickening feet she ran up the twisting passage till she reached the outer cave. Standing in its entrance, she looked toward the hills where she had first seen the golden-haired youths.

It was late summer, and sundown. The magic of the evenshine was over everything, bringing out the glowing purple of the heather, now in full bloom, and all the colors of the great company of moorland flowers. Some blossoms shone like silver dew, others were hardly less blue than the sky that roofed the moor. The skybirds sang above the moor, looking dark against the blue. The peewits called across the heathery spaces. The white-breasted gulls floating in from the sea laughed and wailed alternately as they came.

The gnome maiden was scarcely observant of the beauty now, for the memory of the handsome youths was uppermost in her mind. As her eyes looked across the moor, they were suddenly filled with the sight of two young men striding down the nearest hill. Her heart throbbed against her white side like a bird's, but she did not turn and run into the shelter of the cave this time.

She stood still, watching the young giants' quick advance, then she laughed and ran toward the west, and the giants sped after her.

Tamara ran like a skavarnak, her dusky hair rippling

163

out on the wind behind her. The young men called after her, but she did not stop. She was swifter footed than they, and for all their great strides they could not overtake her.

"Stop, dear maid," they cried; "stay your flying feet that we may hold converse with you."

The gnome maiden only laughed and ran on over the great moor until the young men were exhausted, then she returned to her cavern home unnoticed save by Little Shadows.

Tamara was no longer content to dwell in the underworld, and daily now she stole from the darkness to run in the light. Whenever she emerged from the mouth of the upper cavern, the two young giants, whose names were Tavy and Tawrage, were always in the neighborhood waiting for her to appear. Tamara smiled at them, knowing well that she would have been vexed had they not been there.

She still kept the youths at a distance and whenever they drew too near was off like the wind. Many a chase she led them over the Cornish and Devonshire moors, over the rugged hills and along the cliffs. When they called her by every endearing name in their language and urged her to stop, she only laughed and ran on.

By this time Tavy and Tawrage were both madly in love with the beautiful gnome maiden, but they despaired of ever overtaking her to tell her of their love. Then, one day when their despair was at its height, they found her sitting on a mound on Wooly Barrows under the shadow of a bush.

"We have come upon you at last," they cried, "and we shall not let you escape from us again until we have told you of the love you have awakened in us."

Tamara looked up at the tall young men, smiling into their blue eyes.

They seated themselves on either side of her, and first Tavy, then Tawrage, poured into her not unwilling ear the story of his love. As they were doing this and entreating her to tell them on whom her choice had fallen, her gnome parents suddenly appeared.

The gnome father and mother had missed their daughter and so came to the upper world in search of her. They saw her seated on a bank between two young giants, listening to their words. Filled with wrath, the gnome father cast an enchantment over the youths, causing a heavy sleep to come over them. When they had fallen back on the turf in slumber, he turned to his daughter.

He upbraided her harshly for leaving her dark home and for letting the young men of the hated race approach her, then he begged her to return with him and her mother to their cavern in the interior of the earth. But Tamara refused to leave her lovers.

PIXIE FOLKLORE

"I love this fair upper world," she said, gazing about her from the green bank on which she sat, which being on Morwenstow's highest moor commanded all the country near and far, rugged hills piled with granite, tree-filled valleys, and the great sea, a blaze of blue under the deep blue sky. "I love the sunshine and this free happy moor with its flowers and music, so different from that place of gloom that saw me born. I cannot go back to the underworld even for your dear sakes."

"What do you mean?" asked the gnome father, his face as dark as Morwenstow's darkest cliff.

"I have learned to love the race you hate," Tamara answered tenderly. "I love these fair, strong youths with eyes the color of flowers that break into blossom on the moor. I love every thread of their bright hair which is as yellow as a bush in blossom. I love one better than the other, and that one when he awakes will I choose to be my husband."

"A daughter of gnomes shall never wed with any save a gnome," said the father angrily. "I will turn you into a stream rather than have you wed one of the giant race. Return with us at once to the underworld, or a stream you shall be!"

"I would rather be a stream in this bright upper world than live again in the interior of the hills," said the gnome maiden. "I love the light and these dear sleeping youths.

166

I can no longer dwell in darkness and play with shadows."

The gnome father answered in ever deepening anger, "Then into a stream, O ungrateful daughter, I will turn you!"

Tamara began to weep, and as her dark eyes overflowed with tears she slowly melted into crystal water till there was nothing left of her. Soon, where the beautiful child of the gnomes had sat on a bank of thyme between the sleeping youths, there bubbled a tiny stream. Leaping from the mound, it sparkled in the sunshine and began to trickle down the slope and over the moor like a thread of light, rippling soft music as it went.

"Our Tamara, the fairest of all the gnomes, will be no mother of sons and daughters," moaned the gnome mother as she watched the trickle of water stealing away into the heather.

"That is so," said the gnome father bitterly, "but do not fret your heart because of her. She prefers to be a stream in this evil world than to live beneath it with us. She may be no mother to gnomes, but she will be mother to much beauty. Blossoms will attend Tamara and worship her wherever she chooses to flow along the surface of the world. Flowers almost as beautiful as our beautiful Tamara will bud around her, reflecting their beauty in her water face.

PIXIE FOLKLORE

"By many a bank she will flow, deepening as she gathers strength and power. Her soft water will be a cradle for white lilies. Trees will spring up beside her like magic to shade her from the eye of the sun. Birds will sing to her from their branches, mingling their songs with the music of her waters. Orchards will break into bloom by all her winding ways, and daffodils in their season will look into her crystal eyes with smiles of light, kissing her as she passes onward to the sea."

"But my torn, forsaken heart will never again be gladdened by the sight of my beautiful daughter," moaned the gnome mother, "and Little Shadows will watch in vain for the coming of Tamara. Oh, let us return at once to our home of gloom, for here on this moor I can no longer stay."

"Yes, let us return," said the gnome father sadly now, for he could not turn back the enchantment even had he wished.

When the gnomes had gone, Tavy woke from his sleep. Seeing his brother Tawrage stretched in slumber on the turf and a stream trickling where Tamara had sat, he was full of bewilderment. He hastened away to the tors where his father lived and told him what had befallen him and Tawrage and that the gnome maiden whom he loved was gone but that in her place was a spring of water.

168

THE GNOME MAIDEN

The giant, knowing how he and his fellows were hated by the earth spirits, sensed what had taken place and told Tavy that the gnomes had turned their daughter into a stream because she had refused to give up her love.

"It was your unworthy son Tamara loved," Tavy cried. "Turn me into a stream then, O my father, that I may go and seek Tamara."

Seeing the anguish of his son's heart, the giant granted his request and turned him into a stream which went rushing after Tamara to tell her again of his love.

Tavy did not overtake her until he reached the woods of Warleigh. There, in the green solitudes of faithful lovers, may be heard the meeting of the waters of Tavy and Tamar, the sweet whisperings of love for whose sake Tamara became a stream for Tavy and Tavy became a stream for Tamara.

Tawrage did not waken from his sleep till long after his brother had sped to their father. Seeing a tiny stream, clear as crystal, where he had last seen the gnome maiden sitting and another stream where before there was none, he divined what the gnomes had done. Quickly he rushed away to an enchanter on one of the granite hills and entreated him to turn him into a stream that he might also seek the beautiful gnome maiden.

The enchanter, knowing that the young giant would

never be happy without his brother and the lovely Tamara, yielded to his request.

Tawrage, in his haste to find the gnome maiden, missed his way and, according to the old tradition, is still runing away from the maiden whom he loves. His back is turned to her as he rushes over the rocks and down the valleys in his fruitless search. His voice, still crying for Tamara, may be heard by all who care to follow the impetuous stream along the wild way it takes.

.   .   .   .

Such is the old legend that tells of the streams the Tavy and the Taw, and the beautiful Tamar which separates King Arthur's country from the rest of England.

The Thunder Axe

THERE WAS IN Cornwall a great tin mine called Wheal Glyn that gave employment to many people above and below ground. But there were a few workers in it whom nobody had employed. They were the knockers, whose little pickaxes could often be heard in the old men's learys. No one in Wheal Glyn had ever been fortunate enough to see the knockers except Sampie Tremilling, a tributer, and it happened in this way.

One day, when Sampie was busy near the old men's learys, his work taking him gradually farther and farther away from his fellow tributers, he soon found himself alone. He did not mind this, particularly as he heard just ahead of him the clear knockings of little pickaxes which told him the knockers were hard at work somewhere in the long level where he was working. The farther up the level he went, the more distinct the knockings became.

He stopped to listen and, as he listened, saw a bright light, too bright for candlelight, shining at the far end of the level. Curious to know the nature of this light, he dropped his pickaxe and walked slowly and cautiously along in case he should suddenly come upon a disused

171

shaft. The level was longer than he thought, but the light grew clearer and brighter as he advanced, seeming to compel him to come on. Almost before he knew it, his way was barred by a dead wall through a small round hole of which the light was streaming.

The hole was above his head, but he climbed up and, looking in, saw it was a double gunny. To his huge delight, Sampie saw a score or more of knockers hard at work with pickaxe and shovel. They were proper little miners even to their clothes, Sampie told himself as he watched them working away with all the skill of experienced tributers. In the front of their tiny miners' hats glowed something very soft and bright, but what it was Sampie did not know, only he was certain it was not candlelight. Over their heads was an austull to prevent the rocks from falling down on them.

After a while Sampie turned his glance to the floor of the gunny, which, to his wonderment, was more than half covered with tiny heaps of fire, or what looked like fire. He could not tell exactly what they were, he knew only that they gave no smoke and did not grow less as they burned on the floor, and that each little heap was of different color and brilliancy. Some were red, like the heart of a rose; others were green and more transparent than the waves when the sun shines through them. Some shone white like Cornish diamonds, only with a softer,

172

clearer luster, flashing out not only their own fire but reflecting all the other fires around them.

These tiny fires lighted up the whole gunny and made
it look like the Little People's country, so Sampie declared, while casting a subdued splendor over the busy
miners, who had their backs toward him.

Sampie was so overcome with all he saw that he grew
excited and cried out, "Aw, you little dears in there, dinky
fires an' all!"

No sooner had he given vent to his feelings than there
was a scaval-an-gow among the tiny miners. Then one
of them rushed forward, touched something in the rock
wall, and Sampie suddenly found himself in complete
darkness—the feeble glimmer in his own hat being the
only light in all that long passage. He waited for the light
that had attracted him to shine again. He listened with
his ear against the rock wall for the sound of the pickaxes
within. But no light came, and, as he could not hear anything save the beating of his own heart, he turned back
to his work.

He had been away from it much longer than he had
any idea of, and, when he got back to the place where
he had dropped his pickaxe, he found his pair in great
concern about him. Just as he turned up they were on the
point of going to search for him. The miners were all
eager to know where Sampie had been. When Sampie

told them of what he had seen and heard, they were almost as excited as he was, but one and all they said what a pity it was he should have disturbed the knockers by an unfortunate exclamation.

"Iss, 'twas a pity," said Sampie mournfully.

"I can't make out what they little fires was you saw burning on the gunny floor," remarked one of the miners. "Did 'em give out any heat?"

"I don't think so," answered Sampie. "An' yet, they was brighter than any fires I ever saw."

"I don't believe they was fires at all," broke in an elderly man standing near.

"What was they then, Daddy Vercoe?" asked a dozen miners eagerly.

Daddy was the oldest miner in Wheal Glyn and a great authority on everything pertaining to the mine. If anybody could unravel a mystery or explain away difficulties, it was Daddy Vercoe.

"I believe they was stones, the sort that kings an' queens have got in their crowns, an' great lords an' ladies do wear on their breasts."

"You don't mean for to say so?" cried all the miners, looking at Daddy in amazement.

"Iss I do! An' I'll tell 'ee why I think so. When I was a croom of a cheeld," he continued as all the miners gathered around him to listen, "I heered my granfer tell

174

my father that Wheal Glyn was richer than folks ever dreamed of. You know my granfer was the first to sink a shaft in this here bal."

The miners nodded.

"Well," Daddy went on, "he sank it close to the old men's learys, an' as he was sinking it he came 'pon a gunny an' out of the black wall of the gunny came little sparks of red, blue, an' white fire. Behind them he heered the knockings of little pickaxes an' the sound of falling stones. Says my granfer to himself, says he, ' 'Tisn't tin an' that kind of trade the dinky knockers be after; 'tis stones that have got fire inside 'em.' My granfer was right, you see."

"Iss," said Sampie, "he was. But are they fire stones worth anything?"

"Worth anything, sonnie?" cried Daddy Vercoe with uplifted hands. "Why, bless thy ignorance, boy! One heap of those dinky fire heaps you saw in the old gunny would have made 'ee as rich as a Jew. An' you could have bought up Wheal Glyn herself, if she was up for sale, an' all the country round into the bargain!"

"My dear life, you don't mean for to say so!" gasped Sampie.

"*I do,*" said Daddy Vercoe solemnly.

"What you have lost, Sampie my dear," cried all the

175

miners, turning upon him their pitying gaze. "Why ever didn't 'ee hold thy tongue?"

"How was I to know that them little knockers was a-going to shut up their light an' leave me in darkness?" asked Sampie, ready to drag his tongue out for having allowed himself to give vent to his feelings at that unfortunate moment. "If ever I get the chance of spying upon 'em again, I'll be as silent as a dummie."

"You may never get the chance again, sonnie," put in Daddy Vercoe gravely. " 'Twas a chance of a lifetime. But if ever you do, let me tell 'ee that keeping your tongue quiet isn't all that is wanted to get hold of the little knockers' treasure. They small chaps learned their trade of getting an' keeping when they was Jews.[1] But there is something that *can* circumvent them," he added as Sampie's face showed disappointment.

"What is that something, Daddy?" asked the miners.

"You know, I s'pose," answered Daddy slowly, and Daddy was always very slow when he wanted to impress his listeners as he did now, "that every now an' again we find down by the Jews' works dinky bronze tools with which the old men used to dig the ore out, an' p'raps hit each other with, which we call thunder axes?"

The miners smiled.

[1] NOTE: It is believed that the knockers are the spirits of the ancient Jews who worked the Cornish tin mines in the days of the Druids.

176

"Well," Daddy went on, "if Sampie was to find one of they an' throw it over those little fire heaps, he could have 'em all without asking, an' not one of they little knockers would have the power to prevent him taking their stones."

"Aw, dear," sighed Sampie, "an' I had a little thunder axe in me pocket all the time. I picked it up only this morning, an' I was keeping it for my little brother to play with."

"Keep it in your pocket in case you come upon the knockers again in one of the old gunnies," Daddy advised him. "If you pitch it over them an' their fire stones, you'll be the richest man in all Cornwall!"

Sampie Tremilling was again working one day near the old men's learys, but in a level below the one where he had seen the knockers at work in the double gunny. He was away from his pair, and, as he was shoveling up the rubble into a truck, he heard a rasping noise quite close to him. Stopping to listen he saw a pale, gold-green light like the flame of a glowworm shining out of the darkness about six feet from where he was standing.

"There must be an old gunny close to me, an' I didn't know it," said Sampie to himself. "P'raps the little chaps have come 'pon a gulph of they blazing stones down in this level. If they have I'm a made man, for I've got the thunder axe safe here in my pocket."

177

Taking the little thunder axe, he crept noiselessly up the level until he came to the place from whence the yellow-green light was issuing. It came from low down in the rock where there was an opening about three feet wide. It was the entrance to a single gunny, and Sampie, as he stood and looked, saw against the wall facing him a tiny bench on trestles.

At one end of it sat a dinky man in long robes with a black skullcap on his head and a beard of snowy whiteness flowing down to his feet. His features were pronounced, and his skin was brown as cappry leather. He was evidently a gem-cutter and polisher, for he was bending over a stone that gave out scintillating lights as he tried to cut it while holding it in his hand.

Immediately in front of the strange little man were piles of stones like those Sampie had seen on the floor of the double gunny in the upper level, only they were even brighter and more beautiful. Down the length of the bench were rows upon rows of sparkling gems, blazing with all the splendor of an October afterglow.

For a minute or two Sampie watched with all the eyes in his head. He was about to throw the thunder axe over the bench and its treasures when a sound of voices fell on his ears from the roof of the gunny. Looking up he saw a tiny kibble, the smallest he had ever seen, slowly descending from a hole in the gunny until it stopped close to the dinky old man, who did not turn even to look at it.

The kibble was full of little miners, and when they got out, which they did in perfect silence, they proceeded to empty it. At first Sampie thought it was only rubble, but a second glance told him it was a great deal more than that, for, whatever it was, it was iridescent.

"Like a rainbow all scat to bits!" Sampie exclaimed admiringly to himself.

When the kibble was emptied the little old man sitting on the bench said, without stopping his chiseling, "Is that the last of the sweepings?"

"Yes," answered one of the miners, "it is the last."

"Will you be able to finish that gem before the Time?" asked another knocker, watching the gem-cutter trying to cut something dark out of the stone in his hand.

"I do not know," said the old man hoarsely. "I seem unable to free the knot that prevents its beauty flowing. And it is the most beautiful of all the gems."

"You have been in Wheal Glyn a long while, have you not, O Cutter of Stones?" asked another little miner.

"Yes, since before you were," said the old man with a long-drawn sigh, "and I shall have to be here another century if I cannot loosen this knot before the Time. But go your way, my sons, and tell Her that I have cut and polished all the stones that our ancestors brought to

179

this place from the Land of Burning Stones. They are more than enough to build Her throne, even if I cannot crown it with this, the most beautiful of all."

The miners went up in their kibble, and when they had gone Sampie remembered the thunder axe in his hand. Leaning forward he flung it over the bench and the stones that blazed upon it. It struck the wall behind the bench and as it struck turned over on its edge and fell with a flash like lightning on the precious stone in the old gem-cutter's hands, then dropped at his feet.

The little old man gazed at it a minute and then at the gem, now lying like a globe of flame in his open palm. With a cry that rang through the gunny he shouted, "It is finished before the Time, and the thunder axe has done it! I am free to go the way and to take my beautiful stones of living fire with me."

"Excuse me, little mister," Sampie broke in, "all they beautiful stones blazing away there on the board like a smelting furnace belong to me, an' take 'em away if you dare!"

As his great, rough voice rolled out this bold assertion, the tiny cutter of precious stones rose slowly to his feet, facing the tall, broad-shouldered man. After standing a full minute before Sampie in all the dignity of his minuteness and the gray centuries of his years, he said with a penetrating gaze out of his little black eyes, "How long have my precious stones been yours, pray?"

"Ever since I flung the thunder axe over the board an' you," stammered Sampie, taken aback by the utter calmness of the dinky chap looking up at him with eyes like gimlets. "Daddy Vercoe said I could have 'em all without asking when I had tossed the thunder axe over the fire stones," he added as an inscrutable smile stole over the brown old face uplifted to his.

"Daddy Vercoe was wrong for once," said the gemcutter, stroking his beard, which flowed down all his little length. "The thunder axe you threw has not the power to bind, except at the will of me—its owner. Its special gift is to set free the life imprisoned in the heart of precious stones."

Sampie looked bewildered.

"Without its help I could not have sent this stone's life burning through its veins." The little man looked at the gem in his hands. "I lost my thunder axe long ago and feared I should never find it again. Then one day one of our little miners saw you pick it up. He at once set up a slock-light in the level where you were working in order to draw your attention."

"Aw! was that why they let me clap eyes on the little heaps of fire stones in the old gunny?" cried Sampie, wrathful at being taken in and made a fool of by the sharp-witted little knockers. "An' was that why you set up your green light to slock me here because you did not get your thunder axe back the first time?" he asked more wrathfully as another inscrutable smile swept over the brown, withered face.

"Whatever did you suppose we did it for?" asked the tiny person, still stroking his beard. "It is not our way to show our treasures to a child of an hour, as you are, without a cause. It was *imperative* that I should get back the axe to cut the knot of this queen of gems and to let its beauty flow out before the Time, that I might go my way."

"What do 'ee mean, little mister?" asked Sampie, forgetting his anger in wonderment.

"Ah, *that* is my secret," answered the gem-cutter.

"But can't I have a dozen or so of those fire stones, sir?" begged the miner dolefully, looking with longing eyes at the bench where the scintillating gems were. "I thought I should be as rich as a Jew and have a diggle every day."

"Did you? Well, I am sorry you must be disappointed, but I cannot spare you one of the jewels I have cut and polished. Each one has been done with infinite care and is worth a king's ransom."

"But do 'ee let me have one of the littlest ones to take home along with me just to show that I have seed 'ee polishing stones," pleaded Sampie coaxingly. "I think you might, sir, for I brought 'ee back your little thunder axe, just when you wanted it."

"I am grateful to you for the thunder axe, though you would not have brought it had you known," piped the tiny stonecutter with a curious look in his twinkling eyes. "And to show you that ingratitude is not a fault of ours, I will make you some precious stones from which you may select five."

Turning his back on the miner he began chanting, "Thunder axe, thunder axe, come and help me make stones out of this jewel dust here for the great man miner who brought you hither and threw you over my stones of beauty for his own selfish ends."

The axe, which had lain on the gunny floor all this while, lifted itself at its master's bidding and sprang into his out-stretched hand. The cutter of gems waved it five times over the rainbow-colored dust, muttering in a language Sampie could not understand. In a minute or two, wonderful, irised globes came whirling toward the miner, who watched their coming with amazed eyes.

"Take the five stones you like best," said the gem-cutter, "and remember that each one is worth more than a hundred acres of land. Choose quickly."

It was not an easy matter to choose, as poor Sampie soon found, particularly as each stone seemed more beautiful than its fellows in its dazzling splendor of red, orange, and tender gold, green and violet, wonderful blue.

"Which five shall it be?" asked the miner of himself, kneeling by the stones in a trembling rapture of delight. "Drat it if I can tell," he said, his eyes traveling from gem to gem. " 'Tis hard upon a chap to be obliged to choose."

"Make haste," broke in the dinky gem-cutter.

"It shall be these little beauties," cried Sampie, covering five of the globes of light with his great, grimy hand. "No, it shall be that five nearest your dinky feet, little mister, if 'tis so pleasing to you."

As the miner lifted his hand to lay it over the stones, he found himself in complete darkness. He was too surprised even to light his candle, which had gone out, but when he did so and looked around the gunny he saw that he was alone. The little cutter of precious stones had disappeared and had taken with him all his treasures —rainbow dust, thunder axe, and all!

"What a great buffle-head I was," muttered Sampie to himself when he realized what had happened, "not to have held tight to my riches when I had 'em. 'Twas like letting go the real for the shadow, it was. Aw, Sampie Tremilling, my dear, you'll never in all your born days have such a chance to be rich again."

Needless to say, Sampie never did, nor did he ever see the little knockers again or hear the sound of their tiny pickaxes. And, what is more, Daddy Vercoe declares that the knockers have forsaken Wheal Glyn.

A Brotherhood of Little Shadows

IN THE CLIFFS near Trevone lived a brotherhood of little shadows, each in a ledge of his own facing the west. There were crimson shadows, blue, red, violet, orange; and shadows of all colors and shades, including gray, brown, and black. Each differed from his brother, not only in color and size, but in expression. The dark ones were the Pucks of the shadow world and were as merry as grigs.

This brotherhood of little shadows was very hard working and generally busy as bees from dawn till dark. They did not mind what they did so long as they were of use to someone or something. They held that everything needed a shadow as much as it needed the sunlight, and that not even God's little cow could do without one.

The members of the shadow brotherhood left their ledges in the Trevone cliffs long before the sun began to wheel up behind the Cornish tors and did not return till the sun drew near the western horizon. Then they sat in their ledges and told each other of the work they had done during the day.

187

PIXIE FOLKLORE

One summer's evening the shadows came home as the sun was climbing down the sky and took their seats, gazing thoughtfully out over the sea. It was a glorious evening and the blue air was luminous with light. Behind the sun the sky was an exquisite golden color. The sea which stretched away from the great dark cliffs was almost as beautiful as the sky, and on the burning blue of the heaving water the sun had laid a lane of orange fire. It was a quiet evening. Nothing broke the stillness save the sound of the sea and the waves breaking against the cliffs.

When the shadows had gazed out over the sea a little while, they began to talk to one another, and their voices were soft as themselves.

"Who is going to tell what work he did today?" asked one.

"If somebody doesn't begin soon the sun will have set," said another, "and it isn't so pleasant to tell of the day's service when the sun has gone down."

There was a silence of minutes filled only by the music of the sea and the low thunder of the breakers. Then a little dark shadow lifted up his voice. "I was the first to leave our cliff and that was long before the sun peeped over the land," he said.

"And what did you do with yourself?" chorused the others.

"I found myself in a room in the valley of Crantock

where a poor tired mother lay fast asleep with a baby in a crib by her bed," the little shadow went on. "The babe was wide awake and puckering up her round mouth for a cry when she caught sight of me capering on the wall. The window was open, and the wind flapping the blind helped me to dance. The babe was so delighted that she forgot to cry and watched me till her mother awoke.

"Then, when the babe was washed and dressed, I followed her into the garden, got into a tree, and with the help of Brother Light made flickering patterns on the grass which she tried to catch. That, and a few other small items, made my day's service."

The next to speak was a crimson shadow.

"I found my way into a garden in St. Columb Major," he began. "In front of a rose tree rich in roses and full of bloom and bud sat a young artist. His face was heavy with sadness for he could not get the darkness that he wanted. I felt so glad that I had come and took my place in the heart of the roses and under their petals. The lad was quick to see me and smiling to himself said, 'At last, the crimson shadow that I need has come. I can paint the roses as I want to, now.'

"Catching up a brush he dipped it in crimson and painted as if his very life depended on it. Before the sun was high over our heads he had made a lovely picture of the rose tree—buds, crimson shadow, and all, looking as if you could gather them from the canvas they were so real!"

No sooner had the crimson shadow finished the story of his day's service than a blue shadow broke in.

"I did a similar kindness to a lady artist sitting on a common not a great way from our cliff. She was in front of a large clump of sea holly with something like despair on her face. Like your artist, Brother Crimson, she could not get the effect she wanted and sat gazing down at the sea holly at her feet. Seeing that it was me she wanted, I made my way softly along the holly's blue-veined leaves and cast my darker blue upon them. Then I kept very still.

"When her eyes fell on me her face lit up and, mixing some paint till it was the color of me, she began to paint quickly as if she were afraid that I should go away. I did not go, of course, but stayed with her until I was no longed wanted. Several people came on the common while she was painting. Some drew near and watched her. Some criticized her work saying that the sea holly was quite wrong and that she was putting in colors never seen on the plants. She merely smiled and went on with her work."

The blue shadow turned to a dark shadow sitting near

him and whispered, "Haven't you anything to tell us, Brother?"

The shadow did not answer at once and sat quite still hugging his small soft knee. Then he said, "Yes, Brother Blue, I have something to tell, but I don't know whether the rest of you will find it interesting."

"Leave that to us," cried the shadows together.

"Well then," began the dark shadow, "when I had gained the head of the cliff a white cloud caught me in its folds. We went along till we came to a three-cornered barley field all by itself on the borders of Denzel Downs. The grain seemed tired, and, looking down from the folds of the cloud, I saw at a glance that it was ripening too quickly, for although the heads were golden the stalks were very green.

"A little shadow will do it good, I said to myself; then telling the cloud that I was sure my work lay in the field below, he dropped me inside the five-barred gate. As soon as I could I stretched myself over the satiny surface of the golden grain. It was thankful for my long dark shadow, rippling its thanks when the wind touched it lightly.

"The field was surrounded by a hedge full of July flowers—poppies, cow-weed, and the rest. Yellowhammers had their lodgings there, and they, too, were grateful to me for stretching my shadow over the field and

191

broke into cheerful songs which mingled with the ripples of the golden grain. But it was a very small thing I did."

"The desire to do good is more than the work itself," said a bright orange shadow. "Now, who next will tell of the work he did today? Will you, Brother Black?" turning to a shadow with a face as black as ashbuds in the early spring.

"I shall be very pleased, if you wish to hear my story," returned Brother Black. "When I saw the cloud catch you up," he began, nodding to his dark brother, "I was on my way over the moors in search of work which I did not find till I came to a cottage in the Vale of Lanherne. In the cottage lived an old man and his wife. They were feeble and felt the unusually hot weather very much. As I got close to their cottage window, in front of which stood a great rain barrel, I heard the old man say, 'Shall we go outside and watch the bees? 'Tis piping hot in here, dear heart.'

" 'Not till the shadows lengthen,' the woman answered. 'Sitting in the eye of the sun is hard on an old body.'

"My day's service is made plain to me, I whispered to myself. Climbing up the roof of the cottage I went under the eaves where the swallows flew in and out. Then I began to stretch myself across the front of the house.

" 'It is quite shady outside our window now,' I heard
192

the old man say. 'Come, my dear,' and taking her by the hand he led her into the garden to sit on a bench behind the beehives. I thought as I looked down on them what a pretty picture they made. He had white hair and a face as full of lines as the face of a cliff, and in every line lived a smile. They read from a big book to each other, then talked of what they read. I was so taken up with listening to them that the time passed quickly.

"The day wore on, and I stretched farther over the little garden. They got up from the bench and walked about admiring their flowers. Before a bush of southernwood the old man said tenderly, 'I well remember, my dear, your giving me my first posy of flowers with a bit from this sweet-smelling bush in it. It was your mother's garden then, and I was only a lodger in the cottage. I still have the bit of boy's love, as you know.'

"'And I have the first pansy you gave me,' said the old woman, smiling at him and letting him take hold of her hand. 'You said it was the color of my eyes. What a long time ago that was!'

"I did not leave their cottage till the sun had sunk behind the wooded valley. That's why I was late in getting here," Brother Black finished his story.

"Would any of you care to know what I did today?" a small green shadow put in shyly.

"We would indeed," said Brother Orange, speaking for

all the shadows. "The smallest things are the most important to us."

The green shadow, thus encouraged, began quietly. "All I did was to shadow a fish left behind in Newquay's golden sands. I caught sight of him as I came over the cliffs," he said, "a little streak of flashing light in the clear water. It will need a shadow, poor little thing, I said to myself when I saw it, for when the sun gets up the pool will be almost hot enough to boil it.

"The silver fish rejoiced to see me and quickly flashed into my shadow, which was, not only a shelter from the glare of the sun, but a cloak to hide its brightness from the eyes of the children playing on the sands. I spread my cool green shade over the pool till the sea came in again and covered the pool and the little fish."

Then up spoke one of the biggest of the shadows and one of the most comical looking. He was very thin, all legs and wings like a sparrow just hatched. "You're all such rattle-bags," he said, making a long nose at Brother Green. Then he started talking so fast that he almost ran over his words.

"What I want to tell you is nothing I did today, nor yesterday, nor last week, nor last month, but in the spring of last year. If you hadn't been such rattle-bags, I would have told of my work at that time! Do you remember a day in the middle of May when our cliff and

194

all the cliffs and headlands were one pink glow with thrifts, and the squills flowed down almost to the sea and seemed to us like blue rivulets?"

The shadows nodded. They were not likely to forget that day.

"Do you remember that from the beds of pink and blue milkworts the larks went up singing into the sky?"

They nodded again.

"What I remember is that the beauty of that day made me want to sit here in my seat and listen to the sky-birds' golden music instead of going forth to do my service."

"We remember, Brother Merry," said all the little shadows, "how we upbraided you for wanting to waste your opportunities and how meekly you took our up-braidings."

"So," continued Brother Merry, "after your kindness in telling me my faults, I flipped my way up the cliffs and over the headland toward the north. I felt as frisky as a colt, jumping over the fields and running up the hills, leaping like a spring-heeled Jack. The wind began to freshen and the clouds came down from the tor coun-try in flocks. In a short time I was flying with them, trailing my garments of darkness over the green corn-fields and over the downland where the gorse was a blaze

195

of gold and the fronds of the bracken were shepherds' crooks."

Merry Andrew stopped to make a grimace at his brothers, who could not keep from laughing as he made it.

"That's right, laugh, laugh, laugh, it's good for you," mocked Brother Merry, "only don't laugh like the black-headed gulls! And don't laugh like the silly downs-organ, or he will take you for one and you will have to belong to the Brotherhood of Asses instead of the Brotherhood of Shadows! And don't laugh like a Piskey or you will laugh and laugh till you laugh yourself into one!"

"Don't be so ridiculous," cried Brother Red, "and please make haste. The sun is getting near the horizon and is already making his pathway on the water. If you have a story of work to tell, then tell it."

"Well," said Brother Merrÿ, meekly folding his arms and puckering his face till it was as full of crinkles as an infant poppy, "I flew on at full speed till Brother Wind was in a contrary mood and suddenly stopped blowing. The clouds that had followed me so quickly stopped, too, and hung motionless. But sitting still was not to my liking, and I made my way slowly till I came to a big winding river between rounded hills. On one side of the river were sand dunes, and on the other side facing them a small town.

196

A BROTHERHOOD OF SHADOWS

"I went along the sands till Brother Wind grew tired of being still and blew his horn again, coming up once more from the tor country. I flew over the river then and what a lovely thing it was! all blue one minute and every color the next, as if my Lord Peacock had washed his feathers in it and left the hues behind. When I got over the river, I went up a hill and came to a large white house. As I looked at it I saw a pale face with sad eyes gazing out of an upper window.

"Brother Merry, I said to myself, you are not so full of your fun and tricks but what you can feel for that lad at the window. You must try your best to make him laugh today. Having admonished myself, I went softly till I got into a poplar tree by the house.

"As I lay there under the young leaves I heard the lad say to himself, There isn't a leaf stirring. I am so disappointed. Mother told me that the wind was quite fresh early this morning, just the kind of wind that makes the light and the shadows run races over the hills. When I can watch sunlight and shadows at play, I can almost forget that my legs are no use to me.

"The lad's words filled me with pity, and I felt sorry that I was not the Keeper of the Winds as I would soon have heckled or pinched or done something to make Brother Wind bestir himself. I never so longed before to play at leapfrog with Brother Light. But I was not the

Keeper of the Winds, only a poor little Brother Merry who, although he could say 'gee-up' to most things, had not the power to stir a blade of grass. I felt almost more helpless as I sat in the poplar tree than that helpless lad with the withered legs.

"As I sat quite quiet in the tree I kept one eye on the window where the boy lay and the other on the wind, who had a bad fit of sulks away in the southeast. By the sun's clock it was about an hour to midday and the clouds still hung in soft silvery masses over the land. I could see them from the tree, for the place where the trees were was on high ground. Just as I was thinking that I should not be able to do anything to amuse the child, Brother Wind recovered himself and began to blow hard again. Out from the tree I flung myself, and Brother Light met me as I dropped on to the grass.

"'Will you have a game of leapfrog with me?' I cried to him. 'It is just the wind for it.' Then I whispered to him that there was a suffering lad at the window who would love to watch us play.

"'Gladly will I play with you, Brother Shadow,' cried Brother Light, and off I went, Brother Light after me. He was very quick, quick as his brother the lightning, for one moment he was on the town side of the river and the next on the sand-hill side. But I was as quick as he

198

and leaped over his back, and so we went on, leaping light he and leaping shadow I!

"One moment I took possession of one hill and he the other. The one Brother Light held was all silver sheen, the one that was mine for a moment was as black as a raven's wing. I jumped over his and he jumped over mine. When we got tired of doing that, we ran races, the light after the shadow and the shadow after the light.

"A great company of clouds had by this time joined in the game and ran through the sky. Over hill, over valley, over the river, but never out of sight of the lad at the window, we leaped and ran. The fleecy clouds, like sheep and little lambs, ran with us, and the wind was as merry as any of us.

"By-and-by the sun went westward, and Brother Light followed him. The wind said he was quite played out and went fast asleep, and I made my way homeward. Hither I came by the way of the hill where the white house stood and where the lad still lay at the window. All the sadness had gone from his eyes. By him stood a lady and I heard her say to him, 'Then you have had a nice day, my son?'

"'A glorious day, mother,' he answered. 'The light and shadow have had a game of leapfrog. You never saw anything like it. Every leap was a giant's leap. They chased each other and went like the wind over the river,

199

over the yellow sand hills, over the cornfields, the buttercup fields, over all the land that I could see, even the great tors. My, it was simply grand!'

"I did not hear what his mother said in reply for I was in a hurry to get back to you before the sun sank into the sea."

"We are very glad to hear now of what you did that day," said all the little shadows, their expressions very solemn as they faced the sunset.

The sun had dropped to the sea and was burning like a great round ball of fire. Clouds had gathered above, flushed with crimson and gold, shining like light within light. The sky behind was as white as alabaster lamps when light shines through them. The sea was still one heave and toss, blue as bluebells, and on the ridges of the rippling water sunbeams played hide-and-seek.

The sun disappeared, and only the afterglow burned on in the sky. The shadows were very quiet, and even Brother Merry spoke never a word.